THE ART OF GETTING ALONG WITH PEOPLE

CECIL G. OSBORNE

Zondervan Publishing House
Grand Rapids, Michigan

THE ART OF GETTING ALONG WITH PEOPLE
Copyright © 1980 by The Zondervan Corporation

Zondervan Publishing House, 1415 Lake Drive, S.E.,
Grand Rapids, Michigan 49506

Library of Congress Cataloging in Publication Data

Osborne, Cecil G.
  The art of getting along with people.

  Includes bibliographical references.
  1. Interpersonal relations.   2. Interpersonal
communication.   I. Title
HM132.08   158'.2   80-12832
ISBN 0-310-30612-4

Grateful acknowledgment is made to the publishers of these versions of
Scripture for occasional quotations:

The New Testament in Today's English. Copyright © 1966 by the
American Bible Society. (TEV)

The Revised Standard Version, 2nd ed. Copyright © 1972 by the
Division of Christian Education, National Council of Churches of
Christ in the United States of America. (RSV)

The Living Bible: Paraphrased by Kenneth Taylor. Copyright © 1971
by Tyndale House Publishers. (LB)

Printed in the United States of America

86   87   88 — 10   9   8

Contents

Dr. Cecil G. Osborne may be contacted at the following address:

> Yokefellows, Inc.
> Burlingame Counseling Center
> 19 Park Road
> Burlingame, CA 94010

Preface

How often have you lain awake at night and reviewed, with pain or embarrassment, an encounter that you handled less than brilliantly? Or recalled an encounter that turned out badly? How often have you wished you had rephrased some statement that came out awkwardly? Or thought with sorrow of a relationship that ended disastrously?

Such regrets are a part of the human condition. Yet it is possible to learn to communicate more effectively, and to relate more creatively with others, so as to reduce or eliminate the times of regret.

Jesus devoted a significant part of His teaching to the matter of human relationships. God wants His children to get along well together. As with any other art, it requires study and practice to learn and apply the basic principles of relating well with each other. This book is about the fundamental principles underlying human interaction. You can have a more satisfying life to the degree that you master these basic concepts.

> Patience is the ability to put up with people
> you'd like to put down. —*Ulrike Ruffer*

---

1 • Understanding People in Order to Get Along With Them

A woman once asked a ninety-one-year-old friend why he had chosen to retire to a small Indiana town of five thousand instead of to Indianapolis, where there would be more to do and see.

He replied, "If I were to drop dead one day in downtown Indianapolis, everybody would just step over me and go about their business. If I were to drop dead here, everyone would step over me and go about their business—but they'd say, 'There's old Tom Clark.'"[1]

This man's facetious but apt comment points up an important facet of human nature: *We all want to be noticed.* No one wants to be ignored or forgotten or to die unrecognized.

All humans have a fundamental need to be loved and admired, to be special. The infant longs for its parents' total, undivided love. That deep need, which later lies buried and largely forgotten in the "inner child of the past," never dies completely. It reveals itself in the adult longing for recognition, honors, popularity—any form of positive attention.

Perhaps you have no expectation of becoming world famous, but let your fancy run free for a moment. Fantasy can be fun if it doesn't become a substitute for reality.

How would you like to discover a cure for cancer? Or even for the common cold? That would bring you instant fame—and would benefit humanity.

Would you enjoy being the first astronaut to land on some distant planet? Think of the parades, the adulation, the movie offers, the wealth and popular acclaim.

Would you like to be a famous movie star, or a philanthropist whose name would go down in history? A fabulously wealthy oil magnate, or a wise and renowned presidential advisor shuttling between world capitals to bring peace to a troubled world? A kindly and benevolent judge, handing down wise decisions from the bench? Or perhaps one of the select few in science, art, or literature to win a Nobel Prize?

Such harmless fantasies are a vestige of infancy, when you probably had unconditional love and adoration. But now you are an adult. Pop! The bubble bursts, and you are back to the daily grind, the "is-ness" of life.

WE ALL WANT TO BE IMPORTANT

People have a universal need to be important: if not famous or wealthy, then to have friends who think well of them; if not acclaimed, then at least significant.

You can get along better with people if you will recognize this basic fact and act on it: *Everyone wants to be significant.*

While driving from the San Francisco area to the mountains for my vacation, I stopped at a small-town restaurant for a cup of coffee. An hour out of town, I suddenly realized that I had left my jacket hanging on a hook on the wall. Three weeks later, on my way home, I stopped at the same restaurant. I was not really expecting to see my jacket ever again. But as I walked to the counter for a quick cup of coffee, I glanced toward the wall. There hung my jacket where I had left it.

When the waitress came to fill my coffee cup, she

smiled and said, "There's your jacket over there." Astounded that a waitress would have remembered a total stranger after a lapse of three weeks, I congratulated her on her excellent memory. She smiled broadly and said, "I remembered you."

Every time I think of that town, I remember the waitress with the quick, friendly smile and the fantastic memory. I do not lack for friends. I do not particularly need to be remembered by a waitress in a small-town coffee shop. Yet I still recall that incident with pleasure.

THE NEED FOR RECOGNITION

Every last one of us longs for recognition. All of us, from the president of the United States down to the third assistant janitor in the White House, cherish it. If you remember this, you will relate better to people.

One important way to improve your relationships is to make it a point to remember names as well as faces. This takes a bit of effort, but it is well worth it, for names are important to people. You can remember names if you *write them down* and use some form of word association to recall them.

When you meet a person for the first time, make sure you have the name right. Repeat it a few times during the conversation, and, upon leaving, instead of saying, "It's nice to have met you," make it, "I'm so glad to have met you, Mr. Johnston." Don't trust your memory. Jot the name down if you expect to meet the person again. It takes only a few seconds to write it on a scrap of paper; writing it and seeing it again will impress it on your memory.

THE INFANT GETS UNCONDITIONAL LOVE

Where does our universal need for love and attention originate? It has its roots in infancy.

Generally speaking, infants are loved unconditionally. There is no need for them to do anything but be their parents' beautiful little baby. They are held, cuddled, cooed at, loved, adored, and pampered.

Babies don't have to do anything to earn this love. It is their privilege to be loved and idolized, to survey the world with a wondering, appreciative gaze while held in a loving embrace.

CENTER OF THE UNIVERSE

Of course, infants also believe they are the center of the universe. Indeed, all during infancy they are the center of attention. They cry and someone comes running. They coo and people smile. They play with their toes and people rush for the camera. Everyone admires them.

This is the stage of "infantile megalomania," the babies' feeling that they are all-powerful—which, in a sense, they are during the period of complete helplessness. They are fussed over, placated, catered to. Their every wish is granted.

But what a terrible shock it is when the children discover that this euphoric state is not permanent. Before long they are expected to learn how to walk, talk, and use the potty ("What a trick they played on me with *that* thing!"). Day by day new demands arise; no sooner do the children learn one skill than they must master another. The world is also full of "no-nos" and resounds with, "Don't touch that!"

What happened to that glorious time when the children could do anything they pleased and no demands were made? Once they were constantly adored. Now their hands are slapped when they reach out to touch something forbidden. Or people frown or shout at them. What a disappointing world this is! They have been hit with a great big dose of reality, and the expectations and demands won't cease until they are six feet under.

Inevitably children wonder "Why this sudden change? I had Mother's and Daddy's unconditional love and adulation. Suddenly it's gone. They confuse me with their ten thousand expectations and prohibitions. Now they want me to go to kindergarten, then to school. I have to obey people and do things I don't want to do. They interrupt my play. I was in the Garden of Eden, and I've been evicted."

Then comes the day when the young adults graduate from school. The once-adoring parents are now somewhere back there in the shadows. The young adults are pushed out onto the stage of life without having any chance to rehearse the lines. They aren't even sure of the name of the drama or how it is supposed to turn out. Are they going to make it? They don't know. It's a scary world, with no guarantees. They are, at long last, on their own. In adolescence they longed for freedom from parental constraints. Now that they have it, it can be frightening.

These children-become-adults long for the Elysian fields of infancy—for adoration and unconditional love, to be supremely important to mommy and daddy and everyone else. But that's all in the past now. They have to perform. They are scared—and sometimes lonely. Occasionally they are depressed.

Now begins the lifelong search for success and happiness and fulfillment. These goals have only been vaguely defined for the young adults and they may not have a very clear picture of how to achieve them.

Success seems to mean getting a job, marrying, and raising a family—having two kids, two cars, a cat, and a dog. But in the process of trying to secure these supposed symbols of success, people may get precious little love (praise, recognition, and approval). They are seized with a vague disquietude for which there is no name. They are aware, in quiet moments, of a sense of puzzlement, and have occasional somber moods. Where is all the fun and happiness "they" promised them ("they" being the books and movies and TV programs)? If they pause long enough in their drive for the elusive carrot of success, they have the feeling that something must have gone wrong.

So, the silent cry goes up: *Listen* to me, *affirm* me, *hear* me, *love* me, *touch* me, *hold* me, *talk* to me. I want to feel important, to be significant. This is a universal longing; no one is free of it, though it may be denied and repressed.

The world seems to be made up of three basic types of humans: losers, users, and choosers.

The *losers* are those who, due to an unfortunate mixture of genes and environment, seem incapable of making it in this close-grained world. They grope their way unhappily through life, blundering to disaster.

The *users* are the ones who use other people for their own ends. They may be either facile, gracious manipulators or unappealing and demanding tyrants.

The *choosers* are the people who set their own goals in life, chart their own course, and have enough time and energy left over to reach out to others along the way. They are richly repaid for this, for multitudes are waiting hungrily for that hand, that touch, that recognition. Choosers not only reach their goals; they carry others with them.

JESUS AND HUMAN RELATIONSHIPS

Jesus had a great deal to say about human relationships. The fifth, sixth, and seventh chapters of Matthew (and part of the sixth chapter of Luke) are devoted to the Sermon on the Mount, which deals very largely with human relationships and attitudes.

Psychiatrists James T. Fisher and Lowell S. Hawley write:

> If you were to take the sum total of all the authoritative articles ever written by the most qualified of psychologists and psychiatrists on the subject of mental hygiene—if you were to combine them and refine them and leave out the excess verbiage—if you were to . . . have these unadulterated bits of pure scientific knowledge concisely expressed by the most capable of living poets, you would have an awkward and incomplete summation of the Sermon on the Mount.[2]

Notice how may different aspects of human relationships Jesus covers in those three brief chapters. These are only a few of them:

> "Happy are those who show mercy to others. God will show mercy to them! . . .

"Happy are those who work for peace among men. God will call them his sons! . . .

". . . men were told in the past, 'Do not murder; anyone who commits murder will be brought before the judge.' But now I tell you: whoever is angry with his brother will be brought before the judge; whoever calls his brother 'You good-for-nothing!' will be brought before the Council; and whoever calls his brother a worthless fool will be in danger of going to the fire of hell. So if you are about to make your gift to God at the altar and there you remember that your brother has something against you, leave your gift there in front of the altar and go at once to make peace with your brother; then come back and offer your gift to God.

"If a man brings a lawsuit against you and takes you to court, be friendly with him while there is time. . . .

"You have heard that it was said, 'An eye for an eye, and a tooth for a tooth.' But now I tell you: do not take revenge on someone who does you a wrong. . . .

"You have heard that it was said, 'Love your friend, hate your enemies.' But now I tell you: love your enemies, and pray for those who mistreat you. . . . For he [God] makes his sun to shine on bad and good people alike, and gives rain to those who do right and those who do wrong. . . .

"When you help a needy person, do so in such a way that even your closest friend will not know about it, but it will be a private matter. . . .

"Do not judge others, so that God will not judge you—because God will judge you in the same way you judge others, and he will apply to you the same rules you apply to others. . . .

"Do for others what you want them to do for you."[3]

There is much more in those matchless principles that Jesus enunciated. The Sermon on the Mount is not merely to be read as devotional material; it is intended to be applied to everyday living.

We've learned that there is a universal longing to be accepted and loved. Jesus confirms the principle that manifesting positive goodwill toward people results in better relationships. The conclusion is that we are going to be happier, more fulfilled persons to the degree that we affirm people and show *agape* love. Let's look at some of the steps we can take toward accomplishing that.

Because few people have a well developed sense of self-worth, it is important to affirm them through sincere praise and recognition. I discovered one morning some years ago how little self-worth many people have.

It was a lovely morning, crisp and clear, after a long period of rain and fog. Everyone I met was beaming. "What a beautiful morning!" was the standard greeting.

"Yes," I responded, "and just think, we *deserve* it!"

This comment was met, without exception, by a puzzled, thoughtful silence. Everyone seemed doubtful that they really deserved the beauty of that lovely morning.

Most of us lack some degree of self-worth. Therefore, we do not always feel deserving of good things. Our sense of self-worth, or lack of it, is acquired in childhood. If our parents did not praise and affirm us properly, and criticized us a great deal, we grew up feeling vaguely unworthy. Standards that were set too high, or too soon, generated the feeling, "I don't measure up. I'm not good enough."

Proof of this lies in the difficulty many people have in receiving compliments. In time they learn simply to say, "Thank you." But a majority of people tell me that even though they respond appropriately, it's hard for them to believe that a compliment is sincere or deserved.

GIVING SINCERE PRAISE

Nevertheless, compliments are *always appreciated*. Give praise when it is deserved; don't wait for something extraordinary. Instead of waiting for your share of compliments, be on the lookout for opportunities to give them:

"What a lovely new dress!"

"I really like that new suit."

"What an interesting new hairdo."

"You must give me your recipe for this. It's delicious."

"That was a good job you did."

At a training seminar I was leading, one man stood out in a significant way. He went out of his way to affirm people frequently in a warm, friendly manner. At the conclusion of the seminar I said to him, "You are one of the most affirming persons I have ever known. You recognized people for their comments, for the way they shared, and for their own being."

He smiled gratefully: "Thank you. I do love people."

Look for opportunities to express appreciation to people for who and what they are. Stop waiting for compliments; give them! "Give and it will be given unto you."

John Steinbeck tells of an elderly man who brought home a big bass viol one afternoon. His wife asked, "What in the world are you going to do with that thing?"

"I'm going to play it," he rejoined.

"You can't play an instrument!" she snorted.

But every evening he spent an hour or so with his finger on one string, sawing back and forth, producing a single note. Day after day he played that one doleful sound.

Finally his wife said, "You know, dear, I think that people who play that instrument keep moving their fingers back and forth on the strings."

"Sure," he said disdainfully. "They're looking for the place. I've *found it.*"

When you sound the note of appreciation and affirmation, you've found the key to vastly improved relationships.

Occasionally people object that they feel insincere in paying frequent compliments. This is due to lack of practice. Everyone undertaking a new skill feels awkward at first. But here is the important antidote to that feeling: *It is never hypocritical to say or do the appropriate thing.* With practice you will begin to feel quite at ease in bestowing well deserved praise or offering recognition to people.

EVERYONE HUNGERS FOR PRAISE

Many people believe that too much praise spoils children by making them conceited. But for every child spoiled by too much praise, ten thousand are ruined for lack of it. A typical parent will offer ten or twenty criticisms for every word of praise. The ratio should be reversed.

The same thing applies to adults. People who do not accept themselves, or who may actually dislike themselves, find it difficult to pay compliments. A woman once told me that her husband seldom if ever offered a word of commendation to their children or to her. When she asked him why he never praised anyone in the family, he said, "Everyone is supposed to perform properly without getting patted on the back for it; but when anyone does something wrong, they're going to hear about it from me."

The children were afraid of him and scattered to get out of his way when he came home from work. His wife endured him "for the sake of the children," but added, "The only contribution he makes is to bring home a paycheck. If it weren't for that, I'd divorce him."

Such people were damaged in childhood and seem incapable of functioning as normal parents.

FIVE BASIC PRINCIPLES

Here are five important principles that it might help to memorize:

1. Give pleasure and you will add an important new dimension to your life.
2. People like those who like them.
3. People like those who affirm them.
4. People are attracted to positive, affirming personalities.
5. People like likable persons.

There was a severe business slump, and my friend Mel was worried. Word had gone out that some of the junior executives might lose their jobs. Mel happened to be credit manager and worked directly under the treasurer of the company, a man nearing retirement.

As Mel explained to me, "The treasurer will retire in two or three more years, and he would be the logical one to be let out; but he owns a lot of company stock, and that's an important factor. I could either get his job or lose my own."

I hated to think that Mel might be out of a job, for jobs were scarce just then.

Mel was one of the most cheerful, lovable persons I had ever known. He derived immense satisfaction from making other people happy. He passed out boxes of candy to the office staff on a fairly regular basis. He had a kind word for everyone, from the office boy to the president. He tended to brush off compliments as unimportant, but he passed them out generously and with genuine sincerity.

One day a very relieved Mel reported to me. The board of directors had spent all afternoon debating which official to let go. Finally, one board member said, "Look, we've thrashed this thing out long enough. It's this simple. The treasurer does own a lot of stock. So what? Nobody likes him. Everybody likes Mel. I move we let the old boy go and make Mel the treasurer." The vote was unanimous. And through the years, Mel worked on up the corporation ladder. The deciding factor was that people liked him.

Mel died a few years ago. He is somewhere in heaven making people feel better about themselves, putting his arm around them and expressing great quantities of love and affirmation.

The formula is fairly simple: If people *like* you, other things being equal, you will stand out. If you give pleasure to people, you will get back more than you ever gave. The pleasure principle is ever so important.

Some years ago in a laboratory experiment, some electrodes were implanted in the pleasure center of a rat's brain. By pressing a lever, the rat could activate the pleasure center and get a powerful "pleasure jolt." Upon learning how to press the lever, he did so continuously—without stopping to eat or drink. He kept pushing the lever, getting a total of more than eight thousand ecstasy jolts before he fell over exhausted!

It has been suggested that people would pay almost any price for such a device. The only difficulty is that all work would cease while we pushed the pleasure button. (However, secretly, I think I'd like to try it just once.)

GIVE PLEASURE

A warm greeting, a fitting word of praise or recognition, can give pleasure and make a person feel good all day. Most people are waiting for this, lurking in the shadows of life until some happy, extroverted person comes along to bestow some love. But Jesus said, in effect, "No, no! You have it all backwards. *You* give, and it will be given back to you in good measure. People will pour good things into your life until there is not enough room to receive them."

One of the fastest-growing companies in America has as its slogan, "Find a need and fill it." In human relations the same principle is valid: find a human need and fill it.

Sigmund Freud thought that the sex instinct was the strongest of all human drives. Alfred Adler parted company with him; he insisted that a far deeper need was the drive for significance—the need to be noticed, to overcome one's feeling of inferiority and helplessness.

The controversy still rages. Perhaps the two drives are equal in strength. The important thing is, both are powerful. If you can help a person overcome his or her feelings of inferiority or self-rejection, you become very important to that person, for you have given pleasure.

YOU CAN SUCCEED!

You can be a success! I am not deprecating fame or financial success in the slightest; but those are relatively minor evidences of attainment. A truly successful person is one who has become a loving, affirming individual, one who brings happiness to others.

I think of a woman who had taught school for many years. Upon retirement, she busied herself in church and community affairs. She simply radiated goodwill. I never met her but that I felt better afterwards, for she so sincerely affirmed everyone that it was a pleasure to be around her. She was uncritical. For her, life was too short to focus on the weaknesses of people. She concentrated on their good points. She was an ordinary person with an extraordinary capacity for making everyone else feel good about themselves. Of course, she was greatly admired and loved by all who knew her.

One quite shy young woman who was much too diffident to speak to people in person took to writing them notes of appreciation. I received one once. It said simply, "Thank you for being you. I really appreciate you. Love, ———"

In one issue of our Yokefellows newsletter I had said that I wished that Christmas goodwill could be spread out over twelve months, and that, instead of getting a vast number of Christmas cards, I'd appreciate a note in July, for instance, saying, "I love you." A minister friend of mine who was on our mailing list sent me a handwritten note the next summer saying, "I may or may not send you a Christmas card. But this summer I just want you to know that I do love you." I felt good all day.

Two Alone in a Cathedral

I once had half a day in New York City before my plane left. So I walked from my hotel around the block to St. Bartholomew's, a magnificent Episcopal cathedral. It was empty except for a young black man who was sitting about six rows from the back, on the aisle. I sat several rows behind him for a period of meditation. We two were alone in a vast sanctuary built for a thousand or more. It was good just to "rest in the Lord" for half an hour. I began to feel quiet and in tune.

Finally the young man rose to leave. I too was seated on the aisle, and as he reached my pew, I instinctively reached out my hand. He, just as instinctively, grasped it. Without pausing in his stride he squeezed my hand, and I his. For a fleeting moment in that firm handshake we were neither black nor white, young nor old; we were one in some indefinable, mystical sense. For that moment we bridged the chasm of our separateness. I felt that, though we were strangers, we loved one another, wished one another well; that in Christ we were one.

I remained there in the cathedral for another few minutes. When I rose to leave, I felt a quiet resolve, a new purposefulness, a gentle lifting of some unnamed burden. Something unplanned had planned itself and was working itself out within me, without my directing it. The split second contact with the young black man was the climax of a meaningful half hour of meditation.

Life offers many such moments—swift opportunities to reach out with a word, a gesture, a touch. I regret deeply the ones that I have not seized. There was that lonely, sad-eyed old woman in a cafeteria hunched over a cup of coffee, surveying the world out of hollow eyes. I passed her by without a word, and regretted it as I left. And that frightened young man, staring with a mixture of fear and longing and anger at no one in particular. Why did I not seize the opportunity to reach out with a word or gesture? When I have done this, I have rejoiced. When I have failed to do so, I have felt diminished and saddened by the missed opportunity.

Everyone is laboring under some kind of a burden. When you reach out with understanding and concern and love, you will be the one most richly rewarded. It is worth repeating the words of the Great Giver, the Redeemer of the world, "Give, and it will be given unto you."

There is a way of listening that surpasses all compliments. —*Joseph von Ligné*

2 • Communication: How You Say It

A monk was walking in the monastery garden during a period of meditation. He encountered another monk, who was smoking as he walked slowly along the path.

"Did you get permission to smoke during meditation?" asked the first monk.

"Yes, I was given permission."

"But I asked if I could smoke during meditation and was turned down."

"You didn't phrase it properly. You asked if you could smoke during meditation. I asked if I might *meditate* while I *smoked.*"

How you say it is just as important as *what* you say—sometimes more so.

COMPLETE HONESTY CAN BE DISASTROUS

People who pride themselves on complete honesty, who always say exactly what they think, discover sooner or later that this is the rocky road to impaired relationships. There *is* a time for a blunt, no nonsense ap-

23

proach, a time when the unadorned truth needs to be expressed. In general, however, getting along well with other people requires a more careful and tactful approach.

Sometimes the effort to do and say the appropriate thing backfires.

There is a story about a high school boy who was going out on his first date, to a school dance. His mother was trying to help him over his nervousness before he left. She said, "John, both you and the young lady may be a little nervous on this first date. Be sure to put her at ease."

"How do I do that, Mom?"

"Compliment her on something. That's always appropriate. It will relieve the tension and make her feel good."

After the dance, as John drove the young lady home, he suddenly realized that he hadn't remembered to compliment her. He racked his brain for something nice to say. Finally it came: "Gertrude, for a fat girl you sure don't sweat much."

Good try, poor results.

There is a coffee room in our Burlingame Counseling Center where the office staff gathers during coffee breaks or for lunch.[1] Clients also use the room. Unwashed coffee cups and half filled ashtrays were often left on the table. Signs were posted asking people using the room to empty their ashtrays and put their dirty cups and dishes on the drainboard, but the signs were ignored. Larger notes were posted, without results.

Finally we posted a sign that read: "Due to inflation, coffee will be $1.00 per cup. However, this charge will be waived if you will rinse your coffee cup and put it in the tray, empty your ashtray in the receptacle provided for this purpose, and clean up your own clutter—plus that of any thoughtless predecessor. (Signed) Committee for Neatness and Niceness Opposed to Clutter and Sloppiness."

Staff and visitors took it seriously, despite the facetious phrasing. Things improved dramatically.

A husband who had been seeing me in an effort to resolve a serious marital problem admitted that he had difficulty controlling his temper. He was a perfectionist, a stern disciplinarian with the children, and he frequently lost his temper with his wife. Family relationships were a shambles.

Nothing I suggested made any difference in this man's conduct.

Finally I said, "I don't want you to say a word to any member of your family, at any time, until you have batted your eyes three times. That will give you time to rephrase the statement. Then express your thought with as much tact as you would if you were meeting a total stranger for the first time—someone whom you might never see again. Your family deserves at least as much consideration as you would express to a stranger."

Week after week he reported that he had tried, but simply could not make it work. The irritation and anger slipped out before he could remember the formula.

I said, "Unless you can make it work, I think your wife will divorce you." A month later, she did. He had tried, but not hard enough.

In one session the wife had told me that she loved her husband, but that she simply could not put up with his angry outbursts. He had never believed that she would make good on her threat to divorce him. He was crushed when it happened.

A TIME FOR APOLOGIES

A friend once bought a car from me. When the time came to take possession, he said he would pay me in thirty days. Some months passed without my hearing from him. In the meantime, I moved to another city.

After six months or so, I learned that he had traded the car in on a new one. I was a bit incensed, particularly since I was somewhat short of cash at the time. I wrote him a fairly hot letter asking him in the name of common decency to pay for the car he had disposed of—if not all

25

at once, at least in small monthly payments. There was no response.

A few weeks passed, and I became ashamed of the brusque, peremptory tone I had used. I sat down and wrote my friend a sincere apology. I told him that my offense was greater than the one I had accused him of, and that he could pay me whenever it was convenient.

By return mail came a check for the entire amount he owed me, together with his apology.

I do not offer this example as a formula for getting deadbeats to pay their debts. There is always a chance that you will not get your money without a struggle, or that you will not get it at all. My only purpose in writing the second letter was to clear my own conscience of the guilt I felt over having lost my temper. My cause was just, my hostility inappropriate.

A TIME FOR COMPLETE HONESTY?

How honest should we be? Must we always tell *all* the truth? Jesus once said to the Twelve, "Oh, there is so much more I want to tell you, but you can't understand it now."[2] The disciples would have been confused had he revealed to them truths that were beyond their comprehension.

There is obviously a time to keep still—to say nothing —as when Jesus before Pilate was asked, "Why don't you say something? What about all these charges against you?"[3] Jesus said no more, much to Pilate's amazement.

How much should one confess? Keith Miller dealt with this issue with commendable forthrightness in his regular column in *Faith At Work* magazine. He quotes a letter from a correspondent:

> Dear Keith: I am having real trouble. Sometime ago I heard you speak about honesty, and I realized that I have been a phony all my life. So I decided to change my ways and began to confess to everyone exactly what I feel about them and life. My husband was horrified at some of my past actions which I confessed, and we're not speaking. I am telling the truth, but everything is crashing. Please send suggestions air mail.

Keith Miller answered as follows:

I don't know what you heard me say about confessional honesty, but let me tell you what I intended to say. In the first place, confession of old sins may be healthy and not harm anyone. But there are ways in which thoughtless confession can be very destructive to a relationship. I almost always speak *against* the compulsive type of confession. It's like vomiting on someone—it may make the confessor feel good, but it doesn't do much for the recipient.

Some years ago I spoke about the lack of honesty in my own life at a church group meeting. After the meeting an older man came up and said very thoughtfully, "You really spoke to my condition. I've been dishonest for years and I'm going to change." He seemed to be deeply moved about his decision.

About a month later I got a long distance call. After the operator had identified me, I heard two hostile words from the other end of the line. "You ———!" I was dumbfounded. "Who is this?" It was the man from the meeting. He had gone home and confessed to his wife, among other things, that he had often committed adultery over the years. This was a fact which she had never suspected. "Now," the voice said, "she's under the care of a psychiatrist at a mental hospital. Have you got any more suggestions about Christian honesty, Keith?"

As a result of that encounter I realized in a way that I'll never forget that raw honesty is *not* the highest value in the Christian life, and in fact, that "honesty" can be a very selfish thing, or even a way to clobber people under the guise of being a good Christian. The highest values are love and concern, and one may have to confess some things to God before his pastor, or close Christian brother . . . and not his or her mate which will not destroy their relationship. Alcoholics Anonymous has a marvelous plan to the effect that one confesses his sins to a third party he trusts, not the party he has harmed, and makes restitution to the offended party except when making restitution would hurt that person or someone else.

So although I've experienced and believe in the therapeutic value of confession before a trusted fellow Christian, I try to be careful not to hurt other people just to get it off my chest, and I've made plenty of painful mistakes even trying to follow that rule.[4]

27

The management of a medium-sized manufacturing plant decided to institute an insurance plan in which employer and employees would share the cost equally. The plan required 100 percent participation, but one man resisted the proposal. His foreman reasoned with him, to no avail.

The vice president interviewed the man and explained the advantages of the plan.

"I don't believe in insurance," he protested. "I'm trusting God to take care of me. Insurance shows a lack of faith."

Eventually the president of the firm asked the employee to come to the head office. "Smithers," the president began, "I understand you are a holdout in this insurance plan. You will either sign up or you will be fired. Take your choice."

"Yes, sir. I'll be glad to comply, sir. Where do I sign up?"

The president was astonished. "You've been dragging your feet on this thing for days. The foreman and my vice president reasoned with you, and you still refused. What has changed your mind?" he asked.

"Well, sir," replied the employee, "I just never had it explained so clearly before."

Yes, there is a time for bluntness as well as a time for tact and diplomacy. There are two things that can guide you: the principle of loving concern and the principle of appropriateness. Sometimes only experience or wise counsel can help you decide what is appropriate.

Marie Curling tells of an instance of exquisite tact:

> Jamie was trying out for a part in the school play. His mother told me that he'd set his heart on being in it, though she feared he'd not be chosen. On the day the parts were awarded, I went with her to collect him after school. Jamie rushed up, eyes shining with pride and excitement. Then he said . . . "I've been chosen to clap and cheer."[5]

His teacher had exercised extraordinary tact and loving concern.

Sydney J. Harris writes:

The other evening I met an attractive and not unintelligent woman whose only fault was that she was intolerable. She wanted to be liked and appreciated too fast. She burned out like a firecracker between the soup and the dessert.

One of the most characteristic failings of such people is their desperate need to make an impression. But people need to be unwrapped, slowly and deliciously. Those who tear off their own ribbon and rip open their own covers lose the very appreciation they are trying to win.[6]

The principle here is this: Don't try *too hard* to win acceptance.

"SPEAKING THE TRUTH IN LOVE"

The New Testament employs the beautiful phrase, "speaking the truth in love."[7] We need to do this whether it "works" or not. That is, even if the response is negative, it is always right to apply the love principle in any form of communication.

The wife who says to her husband, "I think it's so stupid of you to sit there night after night, and every weekend, watching all those dumb sports events and asinine cops-and-robbers movies," is not apt to receive a kindly response. She might get a better one with, "Honey, I miss having you to talk to me evenings and over the weekend. I love it when we do things together. Could we plan to go somewhere this weekend?"

"You never take me anywhere," or, "You always do that," are phrases that are best eliminated. These are buzz bomb words, and they are more apt to provoke an angry response or a sullen silence than a fruitful dialogue.

The husband who criticizes his wife's cooking, hairdo, housekeeping—or anything else about her, for that matter—is not going to find her as affectionate as he would if he offered praise occasionally. Criticism is almost always destructive.

An American diplomat who worked on several projects with Madam Nhu, wife of the former president of South Vietnam, wrote of the one fatal flaw in her personality. Though she showed genuine compassion for the people of her country and worked diligently to improve their lot, she displayed a complete lack of tact. She made combative and outrageous statements that were to bring down her husband, his brother, and herself in later years. More people fail in life due to tactlessness than from a lack of ability.

Sometimes parents treat their adult sons and daughters as if they were ten-year-old children. A highly successful business executive in his forties told me that when he went to visit his father for the first time in some months, his father's first words were: "Your hair's too long. Cut it off!" A certain coolness marred the visit.

In Primal Integration therapy we regress clients to various ages to relive traumatic childhood experiences. It is common for the person to reexperience hearing parental putdowns, repeated over and over.

One man kept hearing his mother utter these phrases: "I don't know what will ever become of you"; "Sometimes I wonder why I ever had you"; "You're going to come to a bad end"; "God doesn't love you when you're bad"; "What am I ever going to do with you?" and many similar putdowns.

No parent ever intends for such destructive judgments to be retained by the child's mind, lodged deep in the unconscious; but we now know that nothing is ever totally forgotten. Parental inputs, both positive and negative, become part and parcel of the child's personality.

ANCIENT WISDOM

Aristotle exhorted his fellow Athenians to "be merciful to the weaknesses of human nature; not to consider the actions of the accused so much as his intentions, nor this or that detail so much as the whole story; to ask not what a man is now, but what he has always or usually been . . . to be patient when we are wronged; to settle a dispute by negotiation and not by force."

MANIPULATIVE? OR JUST PRACTICAL?

A group of parents living adjacent to a freeway were alarmed at the recklessness and speed of the drivers. Their appeals to city officials and police brought no relief. At last, after a meeting of the concerned parents, a sign was posted at two nearby intersections: "Slow Down For Nudist Crossing." Traffic slowed to a virtual standstill.

How one expresses something is very important. A friend of mine who was in the business of importing candles found that one expensive item often tended to change from its lovely golden color to a kind of mottled green. He had a few complaints until he began enclosing a printed slip with each of the candles. It read: "Some of our customers tell us that their candles turn to a lovely antique green in time. While we cannot guarantee that this will happen to yours, we can only hope that you will appreciate it if it does."

Purists might criticize the ethics involved in this, but the principle remains valid: How you say it is of utmost importance.

DOING IT WITH MIRRORS

Donald J. White, financial editor of the *San Francisco Chronicle*, has written of an architect who designed a fifty-story building with too few elevators. The tenants were unhappy. They milled around in the new building's marble walled lobby waiting for elevators to take them to their offices.

The building began to get a bad name, major tenants threatened to move out, the owners had nightmares about their multi-million dollar investment going down the drain just because there weren't enough elevators.

They called in a psychologist who specialized in motivational research. The psychologist knew the answer as soon as he had heard the problem, but he waited two months to tell the owners the solution. That made his research worth $7,500. . . .

"Do it with mirrors," he told the owners. "People are more interested in themselves than anything else."

Mirrors were installed in the lobby, where the tenants gathered to wait for the elevators. They managed to wait for up to three minutes for an elevator, while observing themselves, or others, in the mirrors. The building was saved from financial disaster.[8]

BEING POSITIVE WINS MORE POINTS

There is nearly always a better way of saying or doing something. The brutally blunt, "Let's tell it like it is, face the facts, let the chips fall where they may" kind of people get a high score for honesty, but a low one on overall results.

A rather pessimistic man whose personality radiated cynicism, which he mistook for sardonic wit, once said, "I used to respond to almost everything people said with, 'Baloney!' I had no friends and was very lonely. I decided to change. When people would tell me things, I started saying, 'Amazing!' Now I have all kinds of friends." There is power in positive affirmation.

SELF-INTEREST IS NOT EGOTISM

When you see a group picture that includes you, whose face do you look at first? Right—your own. Your reaction may range from "Gee, I look awful," to "H–m. . . ."

It is well to remember that *all of us, without exception, are more interested in ourselves—our feelings, our reactions, our future, how we appear to others—than we are in anything or anyone else.* Your toothache, for example, affects you more deeply than the knowledge that two billion people will go to bed hungry tonight.

Such self-interest does not necessarily constitute egotism or egocentricity. It is simply evidence that we live "inside ourselves." We can feel our own feelings, but we can only vaguely sense the feelings and reactions of others.

In a room full of people, every person is more conscious of what he or she is thinking, feeling, seeing, and experiencing than of anything else. He may be looking about, observing, appraising, talking, but he is still most deeply aware of himself and his own reactions. This holds true for all of us.

It takes extra effort to come "outside ourselves"—to turn our attention to someone else, really listen, and give honest affirmation. To do this is to express caring and concern—which is a facet of love. This happens so rarely that when you do it, you will make a deep impression.

Listen to any two persons talking: usually each is concerned with his own thoughts and feelings or opinions. If you want to get along with people—and here is the crux of the whole matter—*give up your preoccupation with yourself and pay total attention to the other person!*

LISTENING IS AN ART

John MacDonald has stressed the importance of listening as a fine art. He tells of his friend, Meyer,

> who acquires people as easily as a hairy dog picks up burrs. He smiles and listens carefully, and the little blue eyes gleam with good humor and personal interest. He says the right thing at the right time, and surprisingly often the random stranger tells him things he wouldn't tell a blood relative or a psychiatrist. No bore, no matter how classic, ever manages to bore Meyer. It is a great talent, to be forever interested in everyone.[9]

SOME PRINCIPLES FOR BETTER LISTENING

Listening is not just passive hearing. It is an active, participating experience in which you pay genuine attention to what the other person is saying.

Here are some principles that should help you become a better listener:

Don't grab the conversation with, "Yes, now take me, for instance," or, "Yeah, now here's how I see it."

Don't let your gaze wander from the other person's face except momentarily. Give your undivided attention.

Validate the feelings of the other. This calls for something like, "Yes, I see what you mean," or, "I can see why you would feel that way," or "That must have been a great experience. Tell me more about it."

Don't interrupt.

Don't try to top the other person's story or joke. When he or she is telling an anecdote, don't let your mind wander to one *you* can tell. When you do, your eyes glaze over and your attention wanders. You become self-centered instead of an active listener.

Don't criticize. You may be attacking the other person's best friend, religious convictions, or political party.

Ask appropriate questions: "What happened then?" or "How did you feel?" Practice will enable you to find suitable queries.

Don't argue! Arguments seldom settle anything, and they make the other person defensive and even more argumentative. If you are asked your opinion, state it, if it seems important. But let it lie there. Don't make a debate out of the conversation. This is not being mealymouthed or weak and spineless. It is simple common sense.

I recall a very pretty young woman who came to see me about her faltering marriage. Her husband had accused her of being hopelessly argumentative. She said firmly, "My mother taught me to stand up for what's right, and nothing is going to stop me!" She had confused *methods* with *principles.*

I explained to her that it is all right to stand up for one's basic principles—honor, integrity, morality—but very destructive to fight over mere methods, whether to do a thing this way or that. She brushed that aside and wanted to argue with me about it. When I last heard from her, she was divorced, not remarried, and a very bitter young woman.

You Need Not Become a Victim

A woman wrote the following to columnist "Dear Abby" regarding a neighbor who was wearing out her welcome:

This neighbor would pop in on me often, and always without notice. Sometimes I was entertaining a relative or another friend, and frequently I had a lot of work to do, and had no time for a social visit. I became frustrated and didn't know how to tell her without hurting her feelings.

Finally, in desperation, I explained that I really liked her and valued her friendship, but there were times when I wanted to be alone with my friends or family, and as a favor to me to please phone to see if it was all right to come over.

She was very understanding, and thanked me for being honest with her. Now she visits me less often and always phones first. Today we are the best of friends.

In becoming an "active listener," you do not automatically abandon your convictions or lose your identity; you simply learn to focus attention on the other person as an act of caring and concern. It does wonderful things for your relationship.

Wilson Mizner once said that "a good listener is not only popular everywhere, but after awhile he knows something." Calvin Coolidge said, "Nobody ever listened himself out of a job." Considering how vital it is to good human relationships, it is amazing how little active listening is practiced.

DON'T OVERTALK

In my counseling practice I do very little talking. Usually I just listen and, from time to time, ask pertinent questions. Except in those rare cases where an individual is entirely out of focus—suicidal, desperate, entirely lost and bewildered—I offer little advice. Sometimes I ask, "What are your options?" Usually the truth is lodged somewhere within the person's own mind. Questioning and active listening can often reveal the solution deep inside the individual.

Many husbands are poor listeners. One wife complained to me that she listened to her husband when he wanted to talk about his job, "but when I want to share things that are a part of my life, he tunes me out. Sometimes he starts reading the evening paper or turns on the TV. I guess dishes, diaper rash, and drudgery aren't all that fascinating to a man, but I'd feel more loved if he would just listen *part* of the time."

I asked, "Does he ever tell you he loves you?"

"Yes, when he's feeling very affectionate and wants to make love."

"Well," I said, "the next time he tells you he loves you, you might say, 'Tom, I love you, too. But do you know what would really make me feel loved?' He'll ask you what it is. Then tell him that it would make you feel greatly loved if he would take a few minutes a day just to listen—*really listen*—to you. He's no mind reader. Let him know what your needs are."

It worked.

FORMULA FOR SUCCESS

General George C. Marshall once offered this as an important formula for getting along with people:

1. Listen to the other person's story.
2. Listen to the other person's story fully.
3. Listen to the other person's story first.

When Jesus said, "Give and it will be given to you," he was uttering a timeless universal principle. Give your interest, your attention, your concern, and you will get back far more—in time—than you ever gave.

The need for listening is beautifully expressed in the following:

"COULD YOU JUST LISTEN? . . ."

When I ask you to listen to me and you start giving me advice, you have not done what I asked.

When I ask you to listen to me and you begin to tell me why I shouldn't feel that way, you are trampling on my feelings.

When I ask you to listen to me and you feel you have to do something to solve my problem, you have failed me, strange as that may seem.

Listen! All I asked was that you listen, not talk to or do—just hear me.

Advice is cheap; 20 cents will get you both "Dear Abby" and Billy Graham in the same paper.

I can do for myself—I'm not helpless; maybe discouraged and faltering, but not helpless.

When you do something for me that I can and need to do for myself, you contribute to my fear and inadequacy.

But when you accept as a simple fact that I do feel what I feel, no matter how irrational, then I can quit trying to convince you and can get about this business of understanding what's behind this irrational feeling. When that's clear, the answers are obvious and I don't need advice.

Non-rational feelings make more sense when we understand what's behind them.

So please listen and just hear me.

And if you want to talk, wait a minute for your turn—and I'll listen to you.

—Author Unknown

> I can live for two whole months on a sincere
> compliment.   —*Mark Twain*

---

3 • The Importance of
Compliments and Tact

Charlie Brown was talking to little Linus in a "Peanuts" cartoon. He said, "You know that little redheaded girl down the street? Well, I wanted to meet her and talk to her; but I felt so dumb and awkward, and I didn't know what to do. Finally I just walked up to her, and I didn't know what to say, so I hit her."

Many of our inappropriate responses are made because we feel awkward or inadequate.

The art of getting along with people involves learning to be tactful. This involves phrasing a statement or a question in the most diplomatic and appropriate way.

GETTING A SURGEON TO TALK

Once, at a wedding reception, I found myself seated next to a famous surgeon. Though we had never met, I recognized him from his picture, and I had been told a few things about him by one of his colleagues.

I introduced myself, and he grunted a rather unfriendly reply. I commented on the wedding. This elicited a barely audible nod. The prospect of sitting there with this gruff, unresponsive person for the next half hour didn't appeal to me, so finally I said, "Doctor, a friend of mine who knows you well tells me that you have the worst case of bursitis known to medical history."

He turned to me, his eyes shining with pleasure, and said, "Yes, that's true! Let me tell you about it."

For the next forty minutes I was regaled with all the details of his horrendous malady. He told how, in the middle of one critical surgical operation, a sudden excruciating pain had seized him and he had had to have an assistant complete the operation. Though I was not particularly interested in the multitudinous details of his bursitis, I was interested in *him*.

When the reception came to an end, the surgeon gripped my hand firmly and thanked me for being such a wonderful conversationalist. All I had done was to make a brief comment about his bursitis.

A few purists, or legalists, insist that this sort of thing is manipulative, but it should be stated once more that it is never manipulative or hypocritical to *act appropriately*. The surgeon had a need to share his unique symptoms with someone. I felt a need, for the moment, to establish a relationship with a very interesting man.

A man was given a perfectly atrocious Christmas present by his mother-in-law. He looked at it, speechless for a moment, then recovered and said, "How thoughtful of you! This is something I would never have bought for myself, and I know just the place for it!" As his mother-in-law beamed with pleasure, his grateful wife grinned appreciatively. She was sending the message: "Honey, you handled that masterfully, and I love you for it!"

Hobbies As a Conversation Opener

Harry, a friend of mine, was a salesman for a financial service. He once told me that he had tried for many months to get an appointment with a certain bank president. The man refused to see him. Learning that the president was listed in *Who's Who*, he went to the library and did his homework. Among other things, he discovered that his prospect raised pond lilies as a hobby. He then read up on pond lilies. Soon thereafter Harry dropped in at the bank and happened to see the president talking to one of the tellers. When the two had finished their conversation, my friend called the president by name and inquired, "Tell me, what's the market price of pond lilies today?"

The president laughed and asked, "What do you know about pond lilies?"

"Not a great deal, but I'd like to learn something about them."

"Come on into my office. I'd like to visit with you."

They talked for half an hour about pond lilies. Then the bank president said, "Let's see, you represent Standard and Poor Investment Service, don't you? Tell me about your service." Half an hour later the sale was consummated.

Manipulative? Not at all. His prospect had a need to talk about his hobby, and my friend met the need.

How You Say It

To illustrate the importance of proper phrasing, Ken Ruble gives some great examples of how *not* to coin a phrase:

"Your name Doc Livingstone, by any chance?"

"Don't fire until they get awfully close."

"Eighty-seven years ago, our ancestors thought up a whole new thing, liberty-wise and equality-wise."

"We have met the enemy, and they aren't all that tough."

To which one might add:

"I came, I saw, and I really won a tough one."

"Ignore the torpedoes, just keep on going."

These *say* the same thing as the famous originals, but they certainly don't carry the impact.

Bite Your Tongue!

How often have you phrased something awkwardly and wanted to bite your tongue? Don't try to remember all of those instances; it will be too painful. Just learn to prevent such disasters in the future.

Run the statement or question through your mind *first*, then *revise* it so that it sounds just right. Those fifteen billion brain cells work with incredible rapidity. With practice you can learn to monitor and rephrase what you want to say in a split second. Just blink your eyes once or twice, and that will give you plenty of time to come up with a better way of stating it.

A man returning from a not too successful fishing trip carried half a dozen very small fish on a stringer. At the dock he met a fellow angler with a huge fish. The unspoken rule among fishermen is to deprecate your big ones and commiserate with the less fortunate fisherman.

The man with the several small fish, eyeing the big one held by the other man, said, "Just the one, eh?" They both laughed.

For reasons never too clear to many men, most women heartily despise the idea of showing up anywhere in a dress just like another woman's. I recall walking along the street many years ago with my wife-to-be. She had on a lovely new dress. Coming toward us was a young woman wearing an identical one. I thought it interesting and said, "Look, a dress just like yours." Just then the other young woman was abreast of us and said, with a curl of her lip, "I got mine first, dearie." Not good.

A far better response was that of a woman known for her vast wardrobe who encountered another woman at a fashionable party wearing a duplicate of her dress. The two women eyed each other for a moment with a cool, appraising look. Then the first woman, moving closer, said to the other, "I want to congratulate you on your excellent taste." That broke the ice and they both laughed. They then made a joke of the whole thing and called themselves "the twins" during the evening.

How you phrase it is terribly important if you want to get along with people.

How to Win Enemies and Alienate Friends

Here are some ways to win enemies and alienate friends:

1. *"I'll tell you what I think you ought to do."*

This is an insulting assumption of superior wisdom. No one is smart enough to go around telling everyone else what they should do; and if one were sufficiently wise to do that, he or she would know enough not to give unsolicited advice, which is seldom accepted anyway.

2. *"My advice to you is. . . ."*

Same thing.

3. *"The whole truth of the matter is. . . ."*

Really? So you have acquired the ultimate truth? Possibly, but not likely. You're going to be a very lonely person.

4. *"Let me show you where you're wrong."*

Now you're talking to a former friend. Or, if not, to a masochist who loves being beaten down. Intellectual arrogance like that usually springs from a peculiar mixture of ignorance and inferiority.

5. *"I'm only telling you this for your own good."*

Forget it! No one asked you for advice. Who knows what's good for me? I can't do half the things for my own good that I know I ought to be doing.

6. *"Your whole problem, as I see it. . . ."*

More of the same, from an international distributor of arrogance.

7. *"You didn't ask for my advice, but. . . ."*

Stop right there! If I had wanted your opinion, I'd have asked for it. I have wisdom of my own I haven't even used yet.

8. *"Are you saved?"*

No, not really. I'm not completely saved from my fear, resentment, inferiority feelings, and guilt. I resent your asking, though I do appreciate your concern. Jesus didn't go around asking people that question. He did ask, "Would you like to be made whole?" If you happen to know how I can become more whole, tell me! I really want to know.

9. *"Here, let me show you how to do that."*

I appreciate your wanting to help, but I deeply resent your way of phrasing it, as though having some bit of technical skill somehow made you a superior being.

10. *"Now here's how I would have done it. . . ."*

Thanks a lot! I went through a difficult experience, did my best, and blew it. You come along and offer some Monday morning quarterback comments. I don't appreciate your attitude.

11. *"That was a fine talk* (job, meal, flower arrangement, sermon, or whatever), *but there is just this one thing I'd have done a little differently."*

Thanks for nothing. You aren't being helpful, though you may think you are. You are acting superior in an effort to compensate for feelings of inferiority in other areas.

12. *"That's interesting. Now take me, for instance. . . ."*

Watch my eyes glaze over, friend, I just now started to share something, and you grabbed the conversation and intend to hang onto it. No, I won't take you, for instance. I'll take a rain check.

There are thousands of awkward, clumsy, inappropriate phrases. A properly sensitive person will learn from sad experience which ones turn people off.

FANCY TALK VERSUS SIMPLICITY

There is a tendency in our technological society for many people to resort to pseudotechnical gobbledygook in an effort to impress others with their erudition or technical proficiency. For instance, the superintendent of a California school wrote a letter to parents, as follows: "The Oakland Scholars Award Program offers a particular process by which students who demonstrate outstanding qualities of excellence through the talented expression of academic achievement . . ." and so on and on. She is struggling to say that the program is a way of honoring outstanding students. That's all.

Another beautiful example of American technological

babble: "a set of arrangements for producing and rearing children, the viability of which is not predicated on the consistent presence in the household of an adult male acting in the role of husband and father." This gentleman, struggling to sound erudite, is trying to say that Dad isn't home much of the time. Nothing more.

The most succinct and eye-catching comment on that sort of writing I have seen was a bumper sticker that read: "Eschew obfuscation." A writer of bafflegab would make that read: "Insofar as possible, because of the lack of educational opportunities available to some segments of the population, it seems best to avoid utilizing technical language and redundancy in expressing ideas which can be expressed in less complex terminology."

Sometimes guarded language can be used to cloud one's real meaning, as in the case of a man who was filling out a lengthy form in a doctor's office. He came to the part where he was asked to indicate his father's cause of death. He was reluctant to state that his father had been hanged as a horsethief; so, after considerable pondering, he wrote: "My father died at a public function where he was the guest of honor, when the platform on which he stood suddenly collapsed."

Read the Sermon on the Mount in Matthew, or the story of creation in Genesis, or Lincoln's Gettysburg Address and marvel at the beautiful simplicity and brevity of the phraseology. It is usually the small mind with the monumental inferiority complex that uses the biggest words. Say it simply.

Is a White Lie Ever Justifiable?

Many people would insist that they never lie, or only do so on rare occasions. Most would admit an occasional innocent "white lie." But social psychologist Jerald Hellison estimates that the average American lies approximately twenty times a day, including white lies and excuses such as, "I'm sorry I was late. I got held up at the office."

What do you do when you have been served a very ordinary (or even an execrable) meal and feel called upon to say something upon leaving? Can you hedge by exclaiming that it "was a wonderful evening," despite the noise from the kids' bedroom and the pesty dog begging for tidbits throughout the meal?

What do you say when you meet the minister at the church door after hearing a very ordinary sermon? ("Good morning" is quite adequate.)

Upon seeing a new baby for the first time, it is customary to exclaim, "What a beautiful baby!" But what can you say when, as occasionally happens, the infant is quite unattractive? (How about, "Wonderful! You must be very happy.")

What do you say when you visit a friend in the hospital who is obviously dying, or at least looking terrible?

If your home is invaded by a gang of young toughs, should you say, "My husband's upstairs and there is no money in the house"?

Physicians sometimes give placebos (sugar pills) in research projects, telling the subject that they are administering a potent medication. Are such lies justifiable in the interest of science?

In hundreds of daily life situations, absolute honesty would be a disaster.

There are, however, two consequences of deliberate, habitual lying. One is the possible damage one may do to another by giving false testimony. The other is the enormous damage done to the personality of the one who consistently lies. I have known several persons who were pathological liars. That is, they had lied so much that they could not distinguish truth from falsehood. The penalty of consistent liars is that they believe their own lies. Some people lie even when it would be to their advantage to tell the truth.

AVOIDING VERSUS EVADING

Is it ever permissible for a government official to lie, in the interest of national security? Or for a physician to lie when asked point blank by a patient, "Am I going to get well?"

Jesus' example is enlightening. He did not always answer direct questions. He did not *evade*, but He sometimes *avoided* entering into a discussion that would not have been fruitful.

Social Conventions Versus Malicious Lies

There are hundreds of—shall we say, harmless?—lies or minor exaggerations. "I'm *so* glad to have met you." When you say this to someone whom you will never see again, and in whom you have no particular interest, it's an out and out lie. You aren't even a little bit glad. This is just one of countless little socially acceptable exaggerations. The literalist would call it a lie. But translated, "So glad to have met you" means nothing more than, "Hi, shake."

The Power of a Sincere Compliment

John Ruskin, the English essayist, wrote that the greatest efforts of the human race have always been traceable to the love of praise. The reason, of course, is that sincere praise affirms us. It restores our confidence, and—among other things—helps remove nagging doubts about our self-worth.

Jack Denton Scott emphasizes the importance of timing when paying a compliment: "One of the best timed compliments I have heard came from a friend to my wife. He waited until after dinner, just before he left, then said, 'Sometime when you have the opportunity, I'd like to get your recipe for staying slim. I've been thinking about it all evening.' My wife purred for a week."[1]

There is a vast difference between flattery and praise. Flattery has been defined as "excessive praise given for ulterior motives." A compliment is "an expression of appreciation offered with sincerity, with no thought of personal gain." And yet, in a sense, both the giver and the receiver of a compliment gain. The recipient is affirmed, and the giver benefits from the gift, for one always feels better for having bestowed sincere praise.

The biblical statement that it is more blessed to give than to receive might be paraphrased: The one who gives with the right motive gets more of a bang out of it than the recipient.

Children derive their sense of self-worth chiefly from their parents. They have no way of knowing whether they are smart or stupid, pretty or ugly, clumsy or competent except as parents let them know. Unfortunately a typical child is likely to receive ten to fifty putdowns for every bit of praise.

"Look what you did!"

"Oh, for heaven's sake!"

"Leave that alone!"

"If I've told you once, I've told you a thousand times!"

"You're so clumsy!"

"Oh, you did it again!"

"What will ever become of you?"

And on and on and on ad nauseam. A child who receives a steady barrage of criticism almost invariably grows up without a proper sense of self-worth. Criticism creates self-doubt and ultimately results in a deep sense of inferiority.

David, like any normal ten-year-old kid, hated mowing the lawn. (It's always more fun playing, or reading, or watching TV, or just plain goofing off, than sweating over a big lawn on a hot day.) He also hated to rake the lawn before mowing it and to pick up debris that might clog the mower. One hot Saturday afternoon he came into the house with an apprehensive look.

"Dad, the lawnmower got busted."

"Let's go take a look at it."

They did, and Dad discovered that a twig had become wedged between a blade and the striker plate.

"It's not broken, Dave. I'll fix it."

He did, and then said, "Dave, maybe we'd better pick up these twigs the wind has blown out of the trees. They seem to jam the mower." Together they gathered up a score or more of twigs and small branches. Then the father said, "You know, Dave, I do believe this is one of the best jobs of mowing you've done in a long time. It's looking good. And this is the only time the lawnmower has ever gotten jammed."

47

Dave beamed. He had been expecting to get chewed out, and instead he got praise. Thereafter he always carefully raked the lawn before mowing.

PRAISE VERSUS BLAME

It is always more effective to offer praise than criticism. A compliment buys more goodwill than a complaint. People perform better in response to positive affirmation than to a negative comment.

A compliment must not be destroyed by a "but": "That's a nice job, and I appreciate it, *but* there's one thing you didn't do quite right." The "but" takes all the pleasure out of the compliment; it robs it of its effectiveness.

A newly married daughter invited her parents to dinner. She had gone to great pains to make it a very special occasion. As the parents were leaving the mother said, "We had a nice evening, dear, and it was a lovely dinner, except that the roast was just a little overcooked." Of course, that spoiled the evening for the daughter.

Educator John Dewey once said that the deepest need in human nature is the desire to be important. Children who are continually criticized cannot feel important to their parents. They grow up with deep feelings of inferiority.

IT'S MUCH EASIER TO CRITICIZE THAN TO COMPLIMENT

There are several reasons why we humans find it so easy to be critical. First of all, it is a very imperfect world, and there is much to criticize.

I was attending a wedding with my wife, Isobel. No sooner had we entered the church than I was overwhelmed by the atrocious color scheme throughout the sanctuary. I was equally appalled by the architecture. I felt reasonably certain that this large and very expensive edifice had been designed by a committee on the back of an envelope with the stub of a pencil. The colors clashed horribly. The chancel area, if it could be called that, was unbelievably cluttered and crisscrossed with needless angles. I tried to shake my mind loose from its critical attitude and concentrate on the music. That was unfortunate, because the organist wasn't doing too well.

Scarcely moving her lips, my wife whispered, "Pretty awful." And looking back objectively, I can see that we were not being overcritical. It *was* rather bad.

But when the wedding began, I was able to shift my attention from the distracting architecture and clashing colors to the wedding party. The bride was lovely; the ceremony, obviously planned by the young couple, was unique and warm and touching. It was a beautiful occasion, even if the architect and building committee had blundered all over the place.

Yes, there are things to complain about, obvious defects in buildings and people and society. To be oblivious of them would be naive and lacking in discernment. But to be needlessly vocal about them would be inappropriate and destructive.

People have many flaws. Our corrupt society shouts to the heavens of injustice, sin, and the accumulation of major and minor horrors. We cannot ignore these things, but we can avoid developing a carping, critical, negative attitude.

A second and more serious reason we are critical is that we tend to project our own defects onto others. I may acknowledge some of my own faults, but when I can no longer stand the self-criticism, an automatic mechanism known as *projection* goes into operation. I begin unconsciously to see faults in others as a means of justifying my own deficiencies.

I AM THAT PERSON

Increasingly I find myself mirrored in almost everyone I meet. The people I see daily have problems and obvious human weaknesses. But in the dark, on a still night when I am unable to sleep, my ten thousand failures and mistakes tend to appear before me like ghosts from the past. With a kind of perverse tenacity they parade across the screen of my mind; and then, with the clarity induced by relaxation, I see that the faults I have observed in others are but reflections of my own. Their defects are mine, in some degree.

I have not always acted with total integrity; I have not always been completely honest. Perhaps some of my failures have not been as gross or as obvious as this man's, or that woman's, but it may be that I have had greater advantages. I have known the truth longer, cherish it more deeply, and am therefore more guilty, even though my failures may seem less blatant.

In every counselee I see mirrored one of my own defects. I am only different in the degree or specific way in which I manifest the imperfection. I *am* that person.

The most critical individuals are the ones who feel the most self-hate. Critical persons find it difficult to give compliments. They are too wrapped up in unacknowledged guilt and self-condemnation to be aware of the needs of others. They wait in lonely, critical isolation, longing to be affirmed. But it's difficult to compliment a critical person.

SKIP THE ARGUMENT, SEEK POINTS OF AGREEMENT

There are rare times when an argument is almost inescapable. But in general, arguments are fruitless. They build barriers instead of bridges.

A wise man said, "Never argue with an angry woman, a drunk, or a religious fanatic." Or, for that matter, with anyone about *anything*, if you can avoid it. You never learn anything when trying to down an opponent. Nor do you win friends.

I once engaged in a friendly, half-facetious argument with a staff member about something inconsequential. His position seemed so obviously wrong (as the opponent's view always does) that I foolishly continued the debate. Finally he laughed and said, "I can't answer your arguments, but I am still convinced I am right." Most arguments end somewhere on that note—or worse, with both parties convinced that the other is either stupid or intractable. What you do in a typical argument is to cloud the atmosphere with negative emotions, build a barrier, and convince your opponent that you are ill-informed or bullheaded. Is that a goal worth achieving?

If you want to get along with people, *avoid arguments.* This doesn't imply becoming a "Yes, yes, I couldn't agree more" type of person. It means that you are too wise to get drawn into a fruitless argument that neither of you will win.

In the course of a counseling session with a husband and wife, I asked for an illustration of the kind of arguments in which they engaged. After a few moments' thought, they recalled an instance when they had gone to a show and returned home to discover that someone had left the electric stove on under a pot—which had partly melted and smelled up the kitchen. The argument went like this:

Wife: "Oh, for heaven's sake! You left the stove on, and now look at it! We'll never get this smell out of the house."

Husband: "Me? I didn't leave it on. You did."

Wife: "Don't be ridiculous. You were the one who put the water on to make coffee after dinner. Remember? You forgot to turn off the stove."

Husband: "No, I'm sure I turned it off after I made coffee. I used the small burner, and you notice it's the big burner that's been burning for the last three hours."

Wife: "That's not true. You used the big burner, stupidly enough, just to boil a pan of water. You do it all the time."

Husband: "I do not."

Wife: "Of course you do! I've told you and told you!"

Husband: "O.K., have it your way."

Wife: "You're being condescending."

Husband: "No, I'm just agreeing that it is barely possible that I could have left the burner on."

Wife: "Barely possible! It's a foregone conclusion."

Husband (who hates being wrong, but hates worse being dragged into an argument): "Maybe you're right."

Wife: "You don't believe that. You're just trying to pacify me."

Husband: "Could be."

Wife: "That's stupid. You did it and you know you did."

Husband: "Yeah." (He stalked off to the bathroom and closed the door, while she cleaned up the kitchen and threw the ruined pot in the garbage can, fuming.)

Now let's analyze the scene. What was gained? Nothing. She was still convinced that she was right; he was turned off and couldn't or wouldn't talk for two days.

People with weak self-esteem must win an argument at all costs. To lose signifies a loss of identity. A person with a weak identity must always be "right"—or feel degraded. Such a person confuses *opinions* with *self*: "Attack my opinion, and you attack me. Criticize my views, children, house, job, friends, politics, religion, or pets, and you criticize me." Such an individual has little or no identity apart from externals.

In the case of the husband and wife, both lacked proper self-esteem, and each felt they had to win the argument.

People with a strong sense of identity can listen to an attack on their religion, politics, friends, or opinions without feeling particularly threatened. They may be evaluating the critic as ill-informed, "different," or simply an argumentative boor.

What is the proper response to an argumentative person? There are several positive options.

If it is a situation from which you can disengage yourself quickly, just listening with an occasional "H-m-m" can be sufficient. If the encounter seems likely to extend for a long period of time, it is appropriate to ask questions: "You feel, then, that there is an obvious Communist conspiracy to take over the government?" (That is enough to keep the other going indefinitely. The conversation will not lag. Paranoiacs or fanatics—which can be the same thing—seldom lack for words or wait for a response.)

But if you have some strong religious convictions, and someone argues that God is a myth and Christianity is the worst thing that ever happened to the civilized world, you may feel a need to defend your faith. Why? Christianity has been around a long time, and it has survived a host of critics and misguided opponents. It will continue to do so. Your heated defense will not serve the cause of Christianity, nor will it change your opponent's views. "That isn't exactly the way I see it, but I respect your opinion" should be enough of a response. You have staked out your position, and an hour of violent argument will establish nothing except that you got sucked into a futile discussion.

Arguments settle nothing. When a meaningful discussion degenerates into an argument, that is a good time to disengage. Silence can be a devastating response.

Some ministers have as much difficulty with relationships as do members of their congregation. That is one of the reasons why the average pastorate in most denominations is around three years.

There is an oft-quoted statement to the effect that when a new minister comes, the congregation responds with, "Behold him who cometh in the name of the Lord." The second year the reaction is, "By what authority do you do these things?" By the end of the third year, if not before, the cry goes up, "Crucify him!"

It is not easy to please an entire congregation, but some ministers are not adept at establishing creative relationships. They may have studied Hebrew and Greek, learned the names of the nineteen kings of the southern kingdom, and become experts on esoteric matters of church doctrine, but I have yet to hear of a seminary course that dealt with the basics of getting along with people. Perhaps the latter would be somewhat more practical than memorizing all of the names of the places where the children of Israel stopped on the way to the Promised Land.

Ministers are only people, and ordination does not confer on them any particular capacity for being good listeners or for validating the feelings of others. Nor does a seminary degree grant them exemption from the need to be tactful. The effect of a powerful sermon on Sunday morning can be cancelled out by a tactless remark on

Monday, or by a defensive response at a board meeting.

Whether you are preacher or teacher, parent or social worker, truck driver or college professor, business-person, salesperson, or homemaker, your performance can be improved immeasurably by applying some of the age-old principles enumerated in the Bible and validated by human experience.

I could offer a proof text for every method and principle outlined in these chapters, but that seems scarcely as important as the test of pragmatism. Briefly stated, that is the concept that the final proof of a method is whether or not it works. And you will never know whether these principles work until you try them.

From some primal hurt he had acquired a terror of revealing any emotion lest it be construed as weakness, or worse, enthusiasm.
—*Germaine St. Cloud*

After thirty-five years of practice, I ask myself, "What is it women want?"
—*Sigmund Freud*

---

4 • Working Through Differences

If you are old enough to know what a rug beater looked like, you are no longer young. Too long ago to recall without a twinge—is it arthritis or nostalgia?—people used to beat rugs. It is a lost art.

Back in the early years of this century, no one had wall-to-wall carpeting—except, perhaps, the very, very wealthy. They had rugs—nine by twelve, twelve by eighteen if quite prosperous. Vacuum cleaners had not been invented; the very latest thing was the carpet sweeper. So rugs got dirty.

The problem was dealt with by dragging the rugs into the back yard and hanging them on the clothes line. Then one took a rug beater, made of twisted wire in the form of a tennis racquet, and beat the rug until enormous gray clouds of dust rose. They beat those rugs with a vengeance! A year's accumulation of dust floated heavenward as the determined homemaker flailed away. And with it, like as not, went a lot of accumulated anger and frustration that could be released in no other way.

Maybe we can blame the soaring divorce rate on the miscreant who invented the vacuum cleaner. For now there is no rug beater close at hand to swing for an hour or more at a dirty rug; thus, no therapeutic discharge of accumulated indignation. Pure whimsey, of course; yet we all need to have some way of releasing our frustrations.

Golf is a poor substitute; whacking a tiny golf ball once every umpteen yards is pretty weak therapy. Walking is good exercise, and jogging is even better, but they provide only temporary release of tension, at best.

The basic question is, How can husbands and wives —or any person of either sex, for that matter—find satisfying ways of getting rid of accumulated frustrations and resolving differences?

Most Men Hate to Seek Professional Help

The male fear of revealing any emotion lest it be construed as weakness—or worse, enthusiasm—is very great. The individual male ought not to be censured; he is the product of social constraints beginning in early childhood.

"Be a big boy now, stop crying."

"Only sissies cry."

"Be a little man now; dry those tears."

Thus parents coerce boys into believing that tears are a weakness. When tears are turned off, most other emotions are repressed as well.

Adults are permitted to be angry, and even to shout at each other. Little boys are not allowed to get angry, certainly not at their parents. Daddy can shout at Mother and at little David, but David may not get angry and shout at his parents. The psychological law of the land is: "Boys don't feel." Boys are brainwashed into believing that showing feelings is unmanly.

The net result of this is that a majority of men steadfastly refuse to see marriage counselors. "We're adults, we'll handle this ourselves! No one is going to tell me how to run my life," is the male rationalization.

It is the experience of marriage counselors, psychologists, and psychiatrists that at least two-thirds of marriage counseling is initiated by wives. Some therapists put it as high as four-fifths.

This brings us to the matter of husband-wife relationships, and ultimately to the differences between men and women in our culture.

Some feminists play down all but the most obvious biological differences between the sexes and view any other apparent ones as culturally determined. But Dr. Alice S. Rossi, professor of sociology at the University of Massachusetts and an authority on male-female roles in society, takes issue with this concept. She writes:

> There is a tendency to confuse differences with inequality. As far as male and female are concerned, difference is a biological fact, whereas equality is a political, ethical, and social concept. No rule of nature or of social organization says that the sexes have to be the same or do the same things in order to be social, political, and economic equals.
>
> Men, who on the average are taller and stronger . . . than women, generally surpass women in construction work and military combat; women generally surpass men in forming intense emotional bonds with infants and young children . . . [and] the difference has been the basis of the family system.[1]

She points out that not all women have a strong maternal instinct, and that men can become loving, tender fathers. But on the average, "men and women differ in their predisposition to care for infants, and in their ability to learn those caretaking skills. . . . the man's attachment is socially learned."[2]

SEX DIFFERENCES

Let's face it, men and women are different in a number of ways. Here are just a few that psychologists and researchers have documented in recent years:

Men have better daylight vision than women.

Women have more sensitive taste and are more sensitive to touch in all parts of the body.

Men are less sensitive to extreme heat and more sensitive to extreme cold.

Women have better hearing, especially in the higher ranges, and at 85 decibels and above, any sound seems twice as loud to them as it does to a male.

Males, even as infants, tend to be more interested in objects than in people.

Women excel in verbal skills and are better at manual dexterity.

Men excel in a wide range of skills involving the perception of depth in space, an ability that gives them an edge in mechanical skills.

Women process information faster, particularly in tasks (like neurosurgery) that require rapid choices.

Boys are more easily distracted by novel objects, and this, combined with their greater exploratory behavior, suggests a kind of curiosity that leads to success in problem-solving tasks that require manipulation.

Women are more interested in people, and as infants are more attentive to sounds and their emotional meaning.

Men exhibit more daring.

Women are more empathetic.[3]

Many of these characteristics can be seen in infants, and thus one has reason to question the assertion that they are culturally determined.

MEN WHO MARRY THEIR MOTHERS

George and Marilyn* had serious marital conflicts and came to our center for counseling. It became apparent very quickly that George was trying to get from his wife the love that he had never received from his mother. In fact, he was unconsciously trying to make her his mother.

According to a fairly dispassionate description by Marilyn, George's mother was the Wicked Witch of the West—unloving, demanding, and totally unreasonable. George felt that his mother was sometimes a bit unreasonable, but he steadfastly denied that she had not given him love as a child. His behavior showed, however, that

*Names of all counselees are changed, but the stories are true.

he was still trying to win her love, and, failing that, was endeavoring to get it from Marilyn.

I pointed this out to him, but he refused to see it: "No, this is adult love I need from Marilyn. I am no longer a child. It's ridiculous to tell me that my unmet childhood needs are still operating."

George agreed to try Primal Integration to see if he could discover the roots of his problem. In his first session he was regressed to childhood and began to cry in the voice of a small child. He was reliving an ancient little-boy hurt, and pleaded with mommy to love him.

Toward the close of the session, he began to get angry and shouted at her. For some time he beat on the mat, and finally shouted, "I hate you, mommy, I hate you!" Suddenly he stopped, opened his eyes, and said accusingly, "You put that into my mind! You and that rotten music you were playing. I don't hate my mother; she's a fine woman. I don't want any more of this." Whereupon he got up and walked out of the room.

George has been the only person out of hundreds of counselees who refused to go on with Primal Integration therapy once it had begun. He refused to talk about his marriage any further, insisting that he could work it out. The last time I saw his wife, she was asking for the name of a good attorney.

While George's ridiculous behavior is not necessarily typical, it illustrates a problem we frequently encounter: that of a grown man who received little or no love from his mother and expects now to get it from his wife. The frustration and anger he expresses toward his wife is the repressed rage he felt as a small child when he needed love in a form his mother could not give.

ANGER IN MARRIAGE

Emotions are a gift from God. Among them is anger, which is basically a survival instinct. Anger can be *used* destructively, of course. But it is no more wrong to *feel* anger than it is to feel joy or contentment or happiness or loneliness, and to express it appropriately can be a creative act.

59

David and Vera Mace, who founded the Association of Couples for Marriage Enrichment, write:

> Unfortunately, most people know of only two ways to deal with anger—either venting it or suppressing it. Christians in general, and Christian women in particular, have become skilled in "swallowing" their anger, and consider this virtuous behavior. Unfortunately, suppressing anger is like swallowing poison. It makes you ill, and its effects often take a long time to go away. But that isn't the worst of it. Married people who habitually swallow their anger become incapable of being warm and tender. If you choke back negative emotions, you block the channel through which positive emotions also flow. That is why having a fight sometimes enables a couple to be more loving afterwards. But that is hardly the best way to promote love.[4]

The Maces suggest a third way of dealing with anger, which involves three steps. The first is to acknowledge your anger to each other. They point out that it is just as acceptable to say "I am angry" as it is to say "I am tired" or "I am hungry."

The second step is to renounce it. There is nothing of value to be gained in a shouting match. When hostility is vented in angry recrimination, things are usually said which are meant but which are hard to forget or forgive. You can say, "When you do that, it makes me very angry!" but it need not mean that you are going to attack.

The third suggestion offered by the Maces is to ask for help.

> To many, this may seem like weak capitulation. Asking for help is, in fact, a very forceful way of getting the cause of the anger investigated and cleared up. If I tell you I am angry with you and want your help about it, I throw down a challenge. I indicate that I don't mean to fight about it, so you don't have to draw your sword and loaded gun. But I also indicate that I care enough about you to want to work on the anger-producing situation so that a barrier between us can be taken down. And if you accept my invitation, some very creative work is likely to follow.[5]

Half a dozen minor issues can equal a major problem in a marriage. Here are a few suggestions that can bear big dividends.

1. *Be considerate of the other person.*
"Be kind and tender-hearted to one another, and forgive one another, as God has forgiven you in Christ."[6] This verse is usually taught to children in Sunday school; it should be the text of a sermon about every fourth Sunday, for it concerns the problem of all human relationships.

Being considerate involves such simple things as:
"May I help you with that?"
"Here, let me get it for you."
"I'm sorry."
"I was wrong." (This isn't easy to say.)
"Honey, you stay in bed another five minutes. I'll bring you a cup of coffee." (This need not necessarily be an every-morning occasion, but what's wrong with making it an occasional gesture of love? You'd like him or her to do it for you. Why don't you initiate it?)

2. *Husbands could be more considerate and thoughtful in expressing affection, without it necessarily leading to sex.*
This is a universal feminine need, but most men in our culture fail in this area quite consistently.

3. *Both wives and husbands could make an effort to look more attractive for each other.*
A wife who cares little about how she looks while at home does not compare favorably with other women her husband will encounter. An ancient dressing gown or curlers in the hair at the wrong time do little to generate warm and tender feelings.

Likewise, a husband who runs around the house on weekends in a holey T-shirt with a two-day beard is not showing loving consideration.

4. Marriage partners can each show consideration by waiting to unload until the other person is in a frame of mind that is conducive to listening.

If one spouse has had a bad day, it might be a good idea to wait until after dinner to regale the other with his or her frustrations. Bad news is better dealt with when the listener has eaten and is reasonably relaxed.

5. Don't wait for "special occasions" to do something nice for your partner.

If the wife does most of the cooking, the husband can win a lot of points by taking her out to dinner more often. It needn't be a fancy restaurant. Sometimes just going out for a hamburger or pizza can be a relief to a tired, overworked wife. It also shows an awareness of how much work she does in the kitchen and acknowledges that she needs a break from it.

At the same time, a wife shouldn't expect flowers and other surprises without doing some of the same kinds of things for her husband. If he's a baseball fan, she could surprise him with a couple of tickets to see his favorite team play; if he likes music, with tickets to a concert he'd enjoy, and so on.

6. Listen! Just listen, without offering advice, without letting your eyes wander to the TV or the newspaper headlines.

And don't let your eyes glaze over. Force yourself to give attention, for love is not just an emotion; it is an action.

7. Be on time.

An habitually late person is a drag, an imposition, and a social irritant of the first water. Alibis and rationalizations don't work after awhile. Being on time is one way of establishing and maintaining good relationships.

8. Bear your share of the responsibility.

Whether it is housework, tending children, doing the yard work, keeping household records, or whatever, be sure to hold up your end of things. In fact, do your share plus 15 percent. (Add the 15 percent because there will always be that much gap between what you and the other person think you should do.)

BURIED ANGER CAUSES DEPRESSION

Jack's wife was in a mental hospital. Three psychiatrists had assured him that she would never recover. During the several years of her stay in the mental institution she had not shown the slightest improvement. In order to find moral support, Jack joined a men's Yokefellow group which I was leading.

Jack was a physician with a fine practice, a good mind, and a dry sense of humor. He was also a deeply troubled man. He brought up his ambivalence in the group repeatedly. He didn't want to divorce his wife, a hopeless schizophrenic; yet he needed a mother for his small son.

In a properly conducted Yokefellow group one shares feelings, not facts. Advice is not permitted. No one is allowed to say, "You shouldn't feel that way," for we work on the assumption that all feelings are valid. The group members observe the rule of confidentiality: nothing said in the group is ever repeated outside the sessions. Another ground rule involves a goal of thirty minutes a day of reading, meditation, and prayer.

At first our group assumed that the problem was solely Jack's wife's hopeless mental condition. Everyone felt sorry for Jack and compassionate toward Margaret, whom we did not know.

It was some months before we discovered the root of Jack's problem. He fell into the category of the too nice husband. That was both the reason for his wife's mental illness and the fundamental cause of his own deep anxiety.

Jack could smile—sadly—but he never laughed. In fact, he almost never expressed any emotion—anger, love, hate, or fear. He was not devoid of feelings; he had simply buried them so deeply that he was unaware of them.

By having lunch with Jack occasionally, I began to

understand him better. He had a cool, analytical mind and could devastate any statement that he felt was not perfectly logical. He also possessed a calm intellectual arrogance, a judgmental attitude, that surfaced from time to time. Emotions he regarded as quaint and rather ridiculous. He always spoke slowly, and in a kind of melancholy, mildly sardonic manner.

Among other things, Jack shared with me that he had only contempt for the type of books that his wife read.

I began to see why Margaret had gone into deep depression. I could understand that such quiet derision expressed over the years could drive someone first into despair, then into insanity.

It is a psychiatric axiom that you cannot express anger and feel depressed at the same time. Margaret could not express anger for two reasons: she wasn't an angry person, and it would be difficult to get angry at Jack—he was "too nice." But he could be mildly devastating with a pleasant smile on his face. Margaret had simply not been able to stand up to this pleasant, logical paragon of intellectuality. Her recourse was to go into depression, which is usually hostility turned inward.

Jack did well in the group. He regularly spent half an hour a day reading, meditating, and in prayer. He began to understand some things about the human personality that he had never been aware of before. We could sense a gradual shifting from the cool to the warm feeling side of the emotional spectrum.

Jack visited his wife regularly, and though we could only surmise what went on in her mind and emotional nature, the net results were wonderful. Margaret began to improve, and before the year was out she had completely recovered. This, despite the pronouncements of three psychiatrists that she would never be well again. The change in Jack had been the healing factor.

HUSBANDS WHO ARE TOO NICE

The *too nice* husband seldom lets himself feel or express his emotions. Such a man is terribly afraid of his anger, and instead of expressing it he simply glares, or grows rigid and cold, or becomes sardonic. I have known several wives who ended up in a psychiatric ward in response to such husbands. In such instances it is usually the wife who feels at fault and is blamed, while the puzzled husband receives the sympathy of friends and relatives.

The wife of such a man usually experiences guilt for feeling angry or critical. After all, he's such a good husband, and everyone in the community just adores him. He is usually a gracious host and often a pillar of the community; but more often than not he is the one who needs psychotherapy the most.

Roger was a variation on this theme. A very gentle, quiet, and rather timid man, he came to the Burlingame Counseling Center primarily because he had gotten into a brawl in a bar. He had been so worked up that it had required six policemen to get him into a police car. It was not the first time he had been involved in a brawl. Roger was given probation, with the provision that he seek psychotherapy.

It was hard to believe that such a gentle, shy, passive person could have created such a violent disturbance. But in his Primal Integration sessions I began to understand why as he relived the primal hurts suffered in childhood—the innumerable beatings by a sadistic father, abandonment by his mother, and a hundred other assorted childhood hurts.

In primal sessions a person usually experiences childhood hurts first, the Primal Pain.[7] Then comes fear intermingled with the Pain. Next comes anger, the God-given survival response to hurt. In Roger's case the anger, when it finally surfaced, was violent. We provide clients with tennis racquets with which to beat on the mat when angry or frustrated. In one session toward the end, Roger broke two racquets against the wall. They were splintered matchwood when he had finished.

"It felt so good," he said later, "to know that I had permission—when I wasn't drunk—to tell my father off, to scream at my mother, and to get up all that buried anger that has been fermenting down there at the bottom of my emotional structure all these years. I had no idea it was there. Man, that felt great! And now I feel more relaxed than ever before in my entire life. I never knew how tense I was until I discharged all that bitterness and rage. I see now why I have acted with so much hostility toward a number of women I have dated. It became crystal clear in those sessions. It was displaced anger toward my mother."

Roger's gentle passivity had concealed a veritable volcano of repressed rage that had distorted all of his relationships and was threatening to put him in prison. In dealing with it by letting it emerge in safe surroundings and allowing himself to feel ancient hurts, he became a normal instead of a neurotic person.

Many people suppose that just because something happened twenty or forty years ago, the emotion associated with it lies in the past, too. However, we now know, and can demonstrate beyond all possibility of doubt, that even though the event is in the past, the feelings surrounding that event are still in us. If those emotions are unexpressed anger, fear, and hurt, they are doing great damage to us in the present.

One of our Primal Integration trainees, whose own therapy released him from many ancient hurts and neurotic behavior patterns, expressed it beautifully: "Every unshed tear is a prism through which childhood hurts are distorted."

WISDOM FROM "DEAR ABBY"

A great amount of practical wisdom is presented daily by columnist Abigail Van Buren. On two successive days she wrote ten incisive commandments for wives, and another ten for husbands. Here they are:

FOR WIVES

1. Don't keep telling him about all the other men you could have married.
2. Don't bring out the bills at breakfast time.
3. Don't try to start a conversation with him while he's reading or watching a sports event on TV.

4. Don't correct him in front of other people.

5. Don't try to make him jealous.

6. Don't badmouth his relatives.

7. Don't put a shirt in his drawer with a button missing.

8. Don't call him at work unless it's absolutely necessary.

9. Don't use his razor.

10. Don't threaten to leave him unless you have a better place to go.

FOR HUSBANDS

1. Don't ever forget her birthday, your anniversary, Christmas, or Valentine's Day.

2. Don't keep talking about the beautiful chicks at work.

3. Don't pick up something to read when she's trying to talk to you.

4. Don't ever bring a friend home for dinner without asking her first.

5. Don't use her car and return it with an empty gas tank.

6. If you know you're going to be late getting home, *call her* and *tell her*.

7. Don't try to make her jealous.

8. Don't look like a slob all weekend.

9. If you know you're in the wrong, don't be too stubborn to admit it.

10. Don't ever go to sleep without telling her you love her.

Obviously more issues will arise in any marriage than are covered in these twenty bits of marital wisdom. Yet any marriage could be improved by faithfully following those simple instructions.

THE PERFECTIONIST HUSBAND

One husband who would be classified as a perfectionist was married to a much more relaxed, spontaneous wife. On arriving home one evening he stepped into a living room strewn with children's toys, walked past chairs and a table piled high with laundry, and entered a cluttered kitchen. As he surveyed the area, he remarked to his wife, "I wouldn't say the house was untidy, but if the police were to be called they'd say there was evidence of a struggle."

Being a rather uptight individual, this man had chosen a wife who was much more spontaneous and outgoing. She, however, was not well organized, and would drop this to do that and drop that to do something else more interesting. She had unconsciously chosen him because he was well organized and always seemed in control of things.

Now he was feeling, "I wanted a spontaneous person, not a *sloppy* one." And she was feeling, "I wanted someone who would be in charge of things—always competent, but *not* so everlastingly *efficient.*"

The answer to their dilemma, of course, was compromise, patience, and good-natured tolerance, together with an effort to adjust gradually to each other's needs.

A Few Unconscious Reasons Why People Marry Whom They Do

Basically, we marry to get our needs met. But we are seldom fully aware at a conscious level of why we choose a particular person. Here are some examples that are illustrative of the many complex reasons for our choices.

A woman who had a tyrannical father with whom she had a very poor relationship married a very passive man in an unconscious fear that a strong man might trigger her childhood terror.

Another woman who had a seriously impaired relationship with her father married a man with certain physical and emotional traits similar to her father's, in an unconscious effort to relive the unsatisfactory relationship and "make it right."

One young woman who described her father as "absolutely wonderful, loving, tender, and affectionate" married a man who was quite mature and in many ways an admirable person. In her eyes, however, he never quite measured up to her unbelievably wonderful daddy. She spent a great deal of time and energy trying to get him to be a carbon copy of her father. Her efforts drove him to distraction—and very nearly to the divorce court.

A man whose mother was domineering and compulsive married a woman who was warm and affectionate. Never having worked out his buried anger toward his mother, he took it out on his wife and very nearly wrecked the marriage. After eighteen years of marriage he discovered, in intensive therapy, that his excessive anxiety and tension stemmed from his unresolved anger toward his mother.

A very gentle and affectionate man who was given little or no love by his mother married a sweet, passive, frightened young woman who was prepared to do anything he wanted. When she felt courageous enough to go to night school, then to take on an outside job, the marriage nearly broke up. This frightened homebody had grown into a quietly effective, self-assured person who didn't intend to take orders. A substantial amount of therapy was required before the marriage was back on track again.

Marriage—The Most Difficult Relationship

A biographer of Clark Gable pointed out that the actor had had five wives in his lifetime, four of whom had had a total of sixteen husbands in their lifetimes. He had been divorced three times, a widower once, and "a lover too often either to calculate or evaluate." There are still millions of women alive today whose hearts beat faster when they see Clark Gable, the great lover, on the screen.

Unfortunately, excessively handsome men and fabulously beautiful women do not, on the whole, have stable marriages. Good marriages are built on love and companionship and goodwill, on maturity and compromise, on faithfulness and integrity.

Despite the many predictions of its almost certain demise, the American family is in about as good health as it has ever been. As proof, Mary Jo Bane cites the following statistics:

More families have two parents (now 82 percent) than in colonial days (70 percent).

What divorce does to families today, death did in earlier times. As the death rate has dropped, the divorce rate has increased—but most divorced people remarry to stay.

There is no evidence that yesterday's mothers, working from dawn to dusk without labor-saving devices, devoted more time to their children than do today's working mothers.[8]

It is fine to believe in the American family and its future; but I also believe in divorce as a last resort, when it is the only solution to an otherwise intolerable situation. Ann Landers says, "When the marriage goes sour, and there is no love, respect, or loyalty left, I believe it is a mockery to try to hold it together with Elmer's Glue. Or, when one party wants out, for whatever reason, I feel it is best to dissolve the marriage with as much dignity and grace as possible."[9]

I have seen some very sick marriages get well. Sometimes the source of irritation is a money problem, sexual incompatibility, conflict over relatives. These are basically "marital problems," and often they can be resolved relatively easily. But serious personality problems are a different matter. At this point intensive therapy such as Primal Integration is indicated. Surprisingly often, the marriage works when the personality problem is resolved. Whenever there is so much as a glimmer of hope, I believe in trying to make it work.

Mother **feels** the mixture of love and resentment, affection and anger she has for her child, but she cannot afford to **know** it.
—*Nancy Friday*

5 • Getting Along With Children—and How Your Childhood Affected You

It has been said that there are three ways to get something done: do it yourself, hire it done, or forbid your kids to do it.

A young mother was looking at a toy for her child. "Isn't this awfully complicated?" she asked the salesman.

"That, madam," replied the salesman, "is an educational toy designed to prepare the child for life in today's complicated world. Any way he puts it together is wrong."

Children can by turns be wonderful, exasperating, charming, cunning, manipulative, delightful, and maddening.

A brilliant young psychologist wrote a book titled *Ten Commandments For Parents*. Three years after he and his wife had a baby, he revised the book and had it published under the title *Ten Suggestions For Parents*. After they had their fourth child he rewrote it again, using the title *Ten Possible Hints For Parents*.

Recent studies have shown that infants differ markedly from the moment of birth. During the first few weeks some babies are bright, cheerful, and alert, while others seem dull and apathetic. Some of the infants studied slept soundly through the night, while others cried and fretted and awoke at all hours. As they grew older, babies in the group continued to display the same general differences in temperament. The fussy ones continued to cry and whine; the cheerful, "easy" ones were still tractable.

CHILDREN ARE BORN DIFFERENT

There *is* such a thing as a basic constitutional difference between children. Heredity plays a vital part in determining the disposition and general nature of the child. One child loves being cuddled, while another, for no apparent reason, refuses to be held and wriggles down off the mother's lap. Fortunately, the latter are in the minority.

Parents are often understandably confused by a "difficult" child. And even the most amenable of children can pose challenging problems for parents as they mature. Someone has defined a parent as a person who gives lectures on proper nutrition to a kid who has reached six feet two by eating potato chips, cokes, and hamburgers. Being a parent can sometimes be a frustrating experience.

One observer wrote, "Our youth now love luxury. They have bad manners, contempt for authority, and love to chatter in place of exercise. They no longer rise when their elders enter the room. They contradict their parents, chatter before company, gobble up their food, and tyrannize their teachers" (Socrates, fifth century B.C.).

Things haven't changed a great deal since then. But the basic, underlying problem has been intensified by the awesome power of television. A recent study revealed that the average child will see some thirteen thousand violent deaths on TV during the formative years. A five-volume, $1,800,000 report issued by the surgeon general of the U.S. indicates that TV carnage has indeed caused aggressive behavior on the part of many children, confirming what we already knew.

CHILDHOOD BLISS

Many people look back on their childhood as a time of bliss, or at least of unalloyed happiness. Sigmund Freud commented on this:

> When the grownup recalls his childhood, it appears to him as a joyful time, in which one is happy for the moment and looks to the future without any wishes; it is for this reason that he envies children. But the children themselves, if they could inform us . . . would probably give us different reports. It seems that childhood is not that idyll into which we later distort it, but on the contrary children longed through the years to become big, to imitate their grownups. . . . A child is absolutely egotistical; he feels his wants acutely, and strives remorselessly to satisfy them, especially against his competitors, other children, and first of all against his brothers and sisters. I seriously declare it as my opinion that a child is able to estimate the disadvantage he has to expect on account of a newcomer.[1]

Freud's observation is now being validated in a new and startling manner. Through the use of Primal Integration therapy at the Burlingame Counseling Center, we have regressed hundreds of adults back to childhood. They have relived forgotten portions of their childhood, especially traumatic episodes, with as much intensity and clarity as the original events. They are nearly always amazed at the repressed incidents they relive. In the process of reexperiencing those events, they see how their present lives are being affected by them and discharge the anxiety that has encapsulated the traumas.

CHILDREN AND TIME

If it is difficult to be a parent, it is even more perplexing to be a small child. For instance, little children have no concept of time. They have not learned to break down the bounds of their existence into minutes, hours, and days. "Now" for the infant, screaming for its bottle, is forever. There is no past, no future—only the interminable now. Even a child of four has little or no idea what a week means.

When our son was four, his mother once planned to take him to visit his grandmother in Los Angeles, four hundred miles away. For important reasons it became impossible to go on that particular Saturday, so Mike was told that he could go the next week. As far as he was concerned, next week could be in the next century. So, on the Saturday for which the visit had originally been planned, when no one was looking, Mike slipped away to the nearby train station and boarded the first train. (It chanced to be going in the right direction, or he would have ended up in San Francisco.)

He was found some twelve hours later in San Jose, where he was taken from the train and returned to us. A promise was a promise, he felt, and to break it and postpone the trip a week—month, year, century, forever—was a breach of contract.

Few adults reckon with a child's confusion about time and a hundred other adult concepts. Most cannot sense a child's feelings of helplessness or utter lack of comprehension of what may seem to be the simplest facts of life.

Berating a child for not understanding; calling him stupid, thoughtless, unreasonable; or punishing him for failure to grasp adult terms and ideas, is disastrous to the child's personality.

"On the other hand," says child psychotherapist Dr. Haim Ginott, "overprotection is as dangerous as underprotection. Children need to be faced with as much as they can bear as fast as they can take it, for hard knocks are bound to come and they must be prepared for them. . . . Each age and each child can bear some confusion and disillusionment, and a gentle but firm insistence that he face it. This is a fine line but concerned, sensitive parents can find it."[2]

Child psychologists agree on this general principle: If a child feels loved, almost anything you do will be all right. If the child doesn't feel loved, virtually no technique of child rearing will be effective. And one of the surest ways to make the child feel unloved is to keep up a steady, day-by-day barrage of criticism:

"How many times have I told you?"

"When will you ever learn?"

"Oh, for heaven's sake!"

"What on earth is the matter with you?"

"Use your head!"

"Don't you hear me?"

"Do you mean to stand there and tell me. . . ."

And on and on. A continuous diet of criticism, which the child perceives as an attack, will erode his or her self-esteem and cripple him or her emotionally. One result of the loss of self-esteem can be aberrant behavior: "If I can't get their love, I'll get their attention by doing something bad." Continual parental putdowns and criticism can be the root cause of destructive behavior.

CRITICISM IS DESTRUCTIVE

Dr. Haim Ginott has some more sound advice for parents:

> Deal with the situation, not the person. Do not attack him, as happened when Larry, 10, broke a glass. Mother: "What's the matter with you? How many times do I have to tell you to be more careful?" Father: "He can't help it. He's clumsy. He was born that way."
>
> Such criticism attacks the core of the child's personality: his self-esteem. A child may believe his parents and assume the role assigned to him: "Clumsy" will behave clumsily. Recommendation: "The glass broke. We need a broom. The milk spilled, we need a mop."[3]

I recall a family situation that was heartbreaking to observe. An over-talkative, domineering mother and excessively passive father had two children. The daughter was outgoing and spontaneous, but the younger son was pathologically timid and withdrawn. His mother would point to him in public and say, "Clarence is so timid. He doesn't talk much." Whereupon Clarence would draw further into himself and try to disappear. He was obviously suffering agony from his mother's loud announcement that he was somehow not quite normal. I heard her make similar remarks concerning his deficiencies at least a dozen times.

When children lie consistently, it is not because they have decided to become untrustworthy individuals. They have usually learned to do this as a defense against constant accusations or threats.

I can recall as a child how I invariably met any accusation with a lie. Eventually I even lied when it was to my advantage to tell the truth, and then I suffered agonies of guilt over the falsehood. Much later, I learned how an accusatory parent had made me defensive and anxious to avoid punishment.

I also stole things. I didn't know why; I just did. It was not because I hadn't learned the difference between "mine and thine." I always felt appropriately guilty, but guilt feelings seemed a minor penalty when set against the advantage of stealing something. Many years later I learned that I had simply been taking things—often items I didn't particularly need or want—as a substitute for love.

Parents whose children are perpetually dishonest need to ask themselves what they might be doing to provoke such behavior.

A young college dropout who had been sent to me for counseling said, "My parents have always set the standards so high that I couldn't possibly succeed in pleasing them. If I made a B average, they expected all A's. If I got straight A's, they wanted me to get involved in campus activities. I couldn't win, so I dropped out." He was silent for a few minutes.

"My mother always compared me with some of her friends' sons," he continued. "I got the feeling that they were all destined to be on the Supreme Court, walk on the moon, or write best-selling novels. I knew I'd never be good enough to satisfy my mother, so I quit trying. It's useless."

All parents want their children to "succeed." But when the standard is set too high, the child feels that the only way he can win is by failing. One high school boy whose parents struggle with him night after night to get his written assignments ready to hand in on time manages to defeat them by putting his written work in the garbage can on his way to school the next morning.

Don't Expect Instant Change

Sometimes parents who learn more effective principles of child rearing and change their methods are perplexed when there is not an instant improvement in behavior. Perhaps a child has been belligerent or withdrawn, or has been lying or stealing. The fact that the parents have ceased their accusations, or have substituted praise for censure, is no guarantee that the child's personality is going to be altered immediately. Just as it took time for the child to develop those unfortunate traits, it will take time for him or her to relate to parents who have changed their approach.

Haim Ginott says,

> When you know that your child failed a test, do not ask, "Did you pass your exam? Are you sure? Lying won't help. Your teacher told us the truth." Some parents deliberately ask such questions to see if a child will tell the truth—to "teach him honesty." Instead, state, "Your school informed us that you failed the test. We are worried. We wonder how to be of help." Convey to your children that there is no need to lie. You are prepared to listen to bitter as well as pleasant truths.[4]

Sloppy Kids

A certain small percentage of children seem to be "neatniks" from birth. All the rest seem dedicated to the notion that sloppiness is next to godliness. Nagging, cajoling, threats, promises, bribes, a good example—all seem wasted on a child whose life is dedicated to untidiness.

A teenager wrote this letter to columnist Abigail Van Buren:

> "Dear Abby: The answer you gave the mother who had a running battle with her teenage children because they wouldn't keep their rooms picked up is wrong.
>
> I am a sixteen year old boy who came to live with my father and stepmother last summer. Before I came here, I

had to jump from my door to the bed (if I could see it). Now my room is so neat and orderly it looks like the operating room of a hospital.

I fought it as long as I could, but my stomach and my stepmother finally won. I got no breakfast until my bed was made. She put a clothes basket in my closet and nothing got laundered unless it was in that basket. Everything left on the floor went into a "mess box" in the garage, and I had to go there to retrieve it.

I'm glad my stepmother didn't do what you advised other mothers to do, which was, "Say no more. Keep their doors locked, and enter their rooms only to change the beds and make it once a week. When they get tired of living in that mess they'll clean it up." (Signed), Proud of Room and Well Fed.

I would like to meet that wise stepmother. Hers was a much more creative solution than the standard approach. Nagging, complaining, and bargaining are not techniques used in the world at large. Using such methods with a child does not prepare him for life. The stepmother's solution was based on the way the world works—not by threats and bribes, but simply on the basis of cause and effect. In her case she had quietly announced the consequences: "When your bed is not made, no breakfast. When your clothes aren't in the basket, no clean laundry." That is pretty much the way the world operates.

CHILDREN'S ADVICE TO PARENTS

Some of the best advice parents can get is from children themselves. A fourth grade teacher asked her pupils to pretend that they were Ann Landers giving advice to parents on how to raise children. Here are some of the precocious bits of wisdom that resulted:

"Don't always be giving orders. If you suggest something instead of giving a command, I will do it faster."

"Don't keep changing your mind about what you want me to do. Make up your mind and stick to it."

"Keep your promises, both good and bad. If you promise a reward, make sure you give it to me. If you promise punishment, make sure I get that, too."

"Don't compare me with anybody else, especially a brother or sister. If you make me out to be better or smarter, somebody gets hurt. If you make me out to be worse or dumber, then I get hurt."

"Let me do as much for myself as I can. That's how I learn. If you do everything for me, I will never be able to do anything for myself."

"Don't correct my mistakes in front of other people. Tell me how to improve when nobody is around."

"Don't scream at me. It makes me scream back, and I don't want to be a screamer."

"Don't tell lies in front of me and ask me to tell lies to help you out. It makes me think less of you and less of myself even if I am supposed to be doing you a favor."

"When I do something wrong, don't try to get me to tell you why I did it. Sometimes I don't know why."

"Don't pay too much attention to me when I say I have a stomachache. Playing sick can be a good way to get out of things I don't want to do, or going places I don't want to go."

"When you are wrong about something, admit it. It won't hurt my opinion of you. It will make it easier for me to admit it when I am wrong."

"Treat me like you treat your friends. Then I will be your friend and you will be mine. Just because people are related doesn't mean they can't be polite to each other."

SCREAMING PARENTS

One of the most difficult things for children to comprehend is why it is all right for parents to yell at them, but not for them to yell back at their parents. As one youngster expressed it, "I am supposed to show respect for my parents, but they don't respect me. They scream at me all the time. They get mad at me, but if I get mad back at them I am punished, and they say I'm a bad kid. I don't understand that."

Neither do I. There is no less reason for parents to respect a child than for a child to respect parents. In fact, there may be *more* reason for respecting the child, for the child's personality is being formed every day, and a barrage of angry accusations and putdowns creates a neurotic personality.

LIVING UP TO EXPECTATIONS

A group of educational psychologists from Harvard selected an average public school near San Francisco and conducted intelligence testing at one of the grade levels. At random they selected a group of children ranging from the dullest to the brightest and told the teachers that this group comprised *the highest element of intelligence*. A year later they returned and gave that entire grade level another intelligence test. It was found that members of the special group had raised their IQ's an average of two to twenty-five points in that brief time, far in excess of the other children.

This experiment ilustrates well the "theory of fulfilled expectations." The teachers *expected* the "intelligent" children to do well, gave them special attention, encouraged them, and treated them with affection and respect. Even the dullest children in the group responded remarkably well to these expectations. A similar experiment conducted later in Oklahoma confirmed that these results were not unique.

Congruently, the more a child is perceived as being dull or slow and is treated that way, the less motivated he or she is to battle these odds. Many children simply give up and proceed to act out the worst expectation of them.

The "untouchables" in India, when they were regarded with contempt, seemed incapable of rising above the level assigned them. But when Mahatma Gandhi abolished this distinction, many of them proved themselves to be quite capable. Today many of them occupy high government posts.

The same principle seems to have been involved in Jesus' giving Simon the name of Peter ("the Rock"). At a time when Simon was manifesting considerable emotional instability, Jesus said to him, "You are Peter, and on this rock I will build my church, and the powers of death shall not prevail against it."[5] Peter later became the leader of the church in Jerusalem. Of course, Jesus did more than change his name. He accepted him and forgave him, even for his emphatic denial at the end.

TEACHERS AFFECT CHILDREN, TOO

Lest parents be assigned an excessive amount of blame and be made to feel needlessly guilty, it should be emphasized that forces outside the home also figure heavily into a child's development. Chief among these is the school.

Naomi White, a schoolteacher, has shared this:

"I have taught in high school for ten years. During that time I have given assignments to a murderer, an evangelist, a pugilist, a thief, and an imbecile, among others.

"The murderer was a quiet little boy who sat on the front seat and regarded me with pale blue eyes; the evangelist, easily the most popular boy in school, had the lead in the junior play; the pugilist lounged by the window and let loose at intervals a raucous laugh that startled even the geraniums; the thief was a gay-hearted lothario with a song on his lips; and the imbecile, a soft-eyed little animal, seeking the shadows.

"The murderer awaits death in the state penitentiary; the evangelist has lain the past year in the village churchyard; the pugilist lost an eye in a brawl in Hong Kong; the thief, by standing on tiptoe, can see the windows of my room from the county jail; and the once gentle-eyed little moron beats his head against a padded wall in the state asylum.

"All of these pupils sat in my classroom, sat and looked at me gravely across worn brown desks. I must have been a great help to them—I taught them the rhyming scheme of Elizabethan sonnets, and how to diagram a sentence."

The school system, with its ten thousand irrelevant facts and endless lists of wars and kings, must take its share of the blame when things go wrong. Teachers with a class of thirty to thirty-five pupils cannot be expected to make school a source of constant joy; but in many instances they could do a better job. What a teacher (or counselor, or preacher, or parent) *is* can be vastly more important than what he or she teaches.

THE PARENTAL IMAGE

A young man complained to me that his new young wife didn't respect him. I asked how she revealed this lack of respect.

"She won't do as I tell her."

"You feel she should obey you?"

"Of course! That's the way it's supposed to be, isn't it?"

"Tell me how it worked with your parents."

"Dad told Mom what to do, and she did it. He was the boss, like it's supposed to be, and he didn't take any back-talk from either Mom or us kids."

Nothing I could say could convince him that sound marriages are not based on the obedience of either husband or wife. His father, whom he admired and feared, was his role model. His relationships with women were based on what he had seen and experienced in those eighteen years at home. So far as he could see, it had worked with his parents, and there was no other way. He could not accept my view of marriage. His wife divorced him, of course.

The power of a role model cannot be overestimated. What the child perceives in the home and school provides the basis for lifelong patterns of behavior.

A study of teachers revealed that under stress in the classroom they all tended, to some degree, *to deal with the children precisely as they had been dealt with at home when they were young.*

More and more cases of battered children are coming to light, and society is properly horrified at such instances of brutality. Many authorities abhor the idea of any physical punishment at all. But there are exceptions. H. C. Caldwell states:

> A silent swat is worth a thousand words. Our organism is designed to learn by concrete interactions with reality. Ani-

82

mal mothers bat their young around when necessary, and they learn forthwith. Nothing clears the air so quickly for a locked in child as a single swift whack on the rear, just as nothing so confuses, fragments, and disturbs a child as the verbal barrage which passes for "reasoning," or threats.[6]

NAGGING IS DESTRUCTIVE

Nagging destroys a child. Constantly reiterated threats and accusations demoralize any youngster. It is best to condense lectures to three sentences or less; after that, you are talking to thin air. To harp and explain and threaten is to frustrate the child beyond measure.

Kids can do some of the dumbest things imaginable. When I was a child our family lived for several years on a farm at the edge of town. Adjoining the east eighty acres was a woods where I hunted with a .22 rifle and trapped.

One Sunday afternoon I decided to go out and examine a trap I had set in the woods. Mother suggested that I change my clothes. (In those distant days boys dressed up in their Sunday best to attend church.) I assured her that I wouldn't get my clothes dirty.

When I reached my trap, I found in it an inert skunk. A faint odor surrounded the area. Just to make sure that the skunk was dead, I got a four foot stick and poked it. Unfortunately, the skunk's business end was pointed directly at me. Upon being prodded, he came to life and let loose a gas attack. It was awful! I had smelled skunks before, but never at a range of four feet, nor when I was the precise target. The stench was unbelievable.

I wandered around in the woods for half an hour, hoping the worst of it would wear off, and finally walked back to the house. Unfortunately, the wind was behind me. When I was within five hundred yards of the porch where my family sat, I heard my father's yell: "Great balls of fire, son! What happened to you? Go get those clothes off. No, don't go in the house. Go behind the barn. I'll bring you some other clothes."

Even with a bath and fresh clothes, some of the stench remained. I was not welcome to join the others for dinner; I ate alone and pondered my stupidity. Thus do children learn—not so much from admonition as from experience.

I can say to my parents' credit that they never referred to the incident again. There is no need to tell the loser in an encounter with a skunk that he has done something foolish.

IMPORTANCE OF BODY CONTACT

One of the most important aspects of dealing with children concerns body contact. Small children need to be cuddled, held, and touched as often as possible. A bumper sticker asks, HAVE YOU HUGGED YOUR KID TODAY? It's a good question, and the tragedy is that it has to be asked. Small children derive vast comfort and security from being held. Deprived of it, they often feel unloved. Words can never take the place of holding and cuddling.

Of the several hundred people who have had Primal Integration at the Burlingame Counseling Center, a majority have reexperienced the pain of needing more holding. They relive the experience of looking longingly at a parent, hoping that Mommy or Daddy will say, "Come here, honey, sit on my lap."

An oft-repeated scene is this: Little Susie is standing there looking wistfully at Daddy in his easy chair reading the paper. "I want to go sit on Dad's lap, but he's busy. I'm afraid to bother him."

"Can you go ask him?" the therapist asks.

"No, I'm afraid to."

"What are you feeling?"

"Sad, lonely. It hurts because Daddy never holds me. He's too busy. He doesn't love me."

These sentiments are often expressed in various ways by people who have no conscious memory of wanting to be held by Daddy, or of not getting his attention.

Children sense parental love from body contact. They desperately need great quantities of rocking and cuddling to gain a sense of security in a nonverbal manner.

Older children, too big to sit on laps or be cuddled in bed, derive feelings of security and love from a firm, gentle touch, an arm about the shoulder, or a hug just before going to sleep.

RIDICULE IS DESTRUCTIVE

Laughing at a child can be disastrous. It is perceived as ridicule, and small children can be incredibly sensitive to this.

It occurred to me one day that at some point in my childhood I had turned my parents off. I felt my way back to that time to see what had happened and relived a typical event. I had asked some question that to my parents seemed hilarious. They laughed.

I can see now that their laughter was not intended as ridicule, but in my childlike sensitivity I took it as such. At that moment, some voice within said, "I won't ever ask you anything again." And I never did if I could avoid it. I learned from other sources. Partly because of the conflict ("I need to ask, but I won't"), I developed a stutter.

Never, never laugh at or ridicule a child, no matter what the occasion.

Disobedient, unruly children are hard to love. Some children, almost from birth, are difficult to handle, and parents can be driven almost out of their minds by irrational demands and destructive behavior. The irony is that children need love most when they are acting the worst.

Despite alarming evidence of declining morals and violent behavior on the part of young people, it is heartening to learn that this is not the whole story. A recent survey of twenty-four thousand high school juniors and seniors across the United States yielded the following information.

Seventy percent said they had never had sexual intercourse, and a majority named moral standards as a reason for this. Almost half of the students said that they had never drunk beer, and 61 percent had never tried hard liquor. About 88 percent had never used drugs in any form; 85 percent had never smoked cigarettes, and 8 percent had quit.

It needs to be said, however, that these twenty-four

thousand students were chosen by their high school principals, guidance counselors, and organization leaders on the basis of leadership, participation in school and community activities, and academic achievement. In other words, these were the top students.

SPARE THE CHILD

If the marriage is ruined, spare the child. Divorce is increasing at an alarming rate, and when there is a divorce the children are almost invariably hurt.

It is foolish to say that parents should remain together under any and all circumstances for the sake of the children, and equally foolish to insist that a bad marriage is so destructive to children that a divorce is always preferable. Such generalizations are much too broad and simplistic.

Psychologist Marjorie T. Toomin feels that parents should never divorce before the children are six or seven, on the grounds that the breakup of the home creates great insecurity in children. If the mother must take an outside job, she feels, the situation is worsened.

But the ages from six to twelve are crucial, too. If divorce seems unavoidable, the children need to maintain as many roots as possible—to live in the same home (or at least the same neighborhood), attend the same school, and have the same friends.

Some children of divorced parents experience feelings of guilt, believing that they may have been responsible for the breakup of the marriage. One child had disobeyed his father, who soon thereafter left home. The boy wondered if he were the cause of this. Having seen numerous killings on TV, he thought perhaps his father would return and kill him. Other children have the feeling, "Mommy, if you can leave Daddy, you could leave me, too, and what would I do then?"

There are no easy solutions, no pat answers.

The same principle holds true for children of divorce as holds for all other children: If they feel loved, they will not be irreparably damaged by adversity. If they don't feel loved, even minor events can devastate them.

Think of the many ways in which parents deny their children the right to feel what they feel. It is five-thirty in the afternoon and Jimmy, age six, is watching Mother take a pie out of the oven.

"I want a piece of pie."

"No, you don't want any pie now. It's almost dinner time. You can have some for dessert."

Susie, age five, sees something on the toy counter that she wants. Mother says, "You don't want that. It's for older children."

"I want it!" Susie screams.

"Now stop that this instant, do you hear me?"

Jimmy and Susie engage in a pushing match and Susie falls down. Mother says, "Look what you did. Tell her you're sorry."

"She took my candy."

"I did not."

"Susie, tell Jimmy you're sorry you took his candy. Jimmy, tell her you're sorry you pushed her down." Both children scream, "I'm *not* sorry!"

"Yes, you are. Now do as I tell you and apologize!"

In such ways parents refuse to allow children to "own" their feelings. Telling a child not to feel something does not change the feeling; it is still there.

Should mother permit Jimmy to have pie before dinner? Or allow Susie to have every toy she wants? Of course not. But when you tell children to stop feeling as they do, you are asking them to give up ownership of a part of themselves—their own inner experience.

Letting children "own" their feelings does not mean letting them do anything they want. There's a vast difference between stopping an act and dictating emotions. Behavior frequently needs to be limited. We are only talking about the *freedom to feel, not* the *freedom to act.*

In telling Jimmy that he doesn't want any pie before dinner, Mother is asking him to feel as she does. It would be far better to say, "This pie does smell good, doesn't it? I'd like some myself, but we're having dinner very soon, and we'll both have to wait." In this way she validates his feelings instead of repudiating them, but sets limits.

In telling the two children to apologize and to feel sorry for what they did, she is trying to get them to feel what she thinks they ought to feel. This is a denial of their legitimate feelings. Susie wanted some of Jimmy's candy (a valid feeling) and Jimmy was outraged when she took it (also a perfectly legitimate feeling). The mother was dictating what they *should* feel, and making them feel guilty for having some perfectly normal emotions. The mother would do much better to say:

"Susie, I know you wanted some candy. I understand that. But you ate all of yours, then grabbed Jimmy's. We don't allow that. And Jimmy, I know you didn't like it when Susie took your candy, but it is not permitted to push or hit someone." In ten minutes or less they would be playing together happily, and "owning" their feelings.[7]

Many youngsters turn their hostility against themselves with asthma, vomiting, continual accidents, and exaggerated fears. The overly "good" and extremely shy child often masks strong aggression that he or she has learned is unacceptable. Such a child steers clear of involvement with others so that the secret won't leak out.

Dorothy C. Briggs has observed that

> the child who is taught that hostility brings disapproval becomes frightened of his own aggressive impulses. Youngsters under six believe that aggressive wishes—that the baby would disappear, for example—will become facts. They may be overly sweet to deny their wishes to themselves and others. The difference between reality and fancy is hazy to the small child. Even when he doesn't put his aggressive wishes into acts, he believes he is "bad." You have to actively teach the difference between hostile feelings and hostile acts.[8]

The art of understanding children, including your own inner child of the past, can be mastered. It requires some time and effort, but it is an art that will be richly rewarded.

They are the true disciples of Christ, not who
know most, but who love most.
—*Frederick Sponheim the Elder*

6 • Getting Along With Neurotics

There is, of course, a clear-cut distinction between a
neurotic and a psychotic. It has been said that a
psychotic thinks two and two are five, whereas a neurotic
knows two and two are four and hates it. Another oft-
quoted attempt to clarify the distinction has it that a
neurotic builds air castles, the psychotic lives in them,
and the psychiatrist collects the rent.

A psychotic is a person who is out of touch with reality.
A neurotic is one who consistently *feels or does something to excess.* Excessiveness is the mark of the neurotic.

THE WORKAHOLIC

Don was a compulsive worker. He spent an hour and a
half daily commuting, put in eight hours at the office,
brought a briefcase home from the office, and worked an
hour or two each evening. He planned vacations, but
something nearly always interfered. When he did man-
age to take some time off, he wasn't really relaxed.
Nothing made him content except work.

The origin of this neurosis could be any number of things: demanding or perfectionistic parents; a deep-seated sense of insecurity and inferiority, for which he compensates by achieving; a strong but partially repressed sense of guilt, or any combination of these. There are numerous other possibilities.

How do you deal with a compulsive worker? Reasoning with such a person is worse than futile. The problem is not with his thinking, but with his emotions; and emotions do not respond to logic.

There is literally nothing you can say or do that is likely to change such a person. A man like Don may point out that he is "doing it all for the family," to "get ahead." The workaholic will always find some rationalization for his or her excessiveness.

Long-term therapy is the only answer. But talk therapy usually does not resolve such problems, since *virtually all excessiveness is rooted in childhood*. Intensive therapy such as Primal Integration is usually indicated. Of course, the compulsive worker seldom sees a need for therapy. A workaholic has one of the few neuroses that can pass for a virtue in the eyes of society.

THE PERFECTIONIST

Fred was compulsively perfectionistic. His desk and drawers were very neat, as were his clothes, workbench, and car. Everything about him was orderly. He became irritable or very anxious if things weren't properly organized.

Usually such a man is married to a much more relaxed wife; and when the perfectionist is a woman, she is almost always married to a more relaxed husband. Unconsciously, the perfectionist seeks a marriage partner who is not so uptight; and the very relaxed individual unconsciously searches for a more orderly person.

Ted's wife complained to me that he criticized the way she ate corn on the cob.

"How does he want you to do it?"

"I eat it lengthwise. He insists I should eat in a circular

manner, going round and round the cob, which he says is neater and more efficient."

I told Ted to save his perfectionistic suggestions for the office, where he deals in decimals and technical matters all day. He tried, but inwardly he was bothered by his wife's more relaxed personality.

One husband made the mistake of rearranging his wife's entire kitchen while she was away for a few days. It took her three days to get over her indignation and bring the kitchen back to normal. I told him in a counseling session to stay out of the kitchen unless invited in, and to let her make all final decisions concerning furnishings, decorating, and other arrangements around the home.

"I just wanted to be helpful," he said.

"Don't mess with her nest," I replied, "or you will be in trouble."

As with the workaholic, nagging or logic seldom make any difference with the perfectionist. He or she may be induced to stop complaining about whatever it is that isn't shipshape, but it will be by an act of the will. He or she has not changed inwardly.

THE COMPULSIVE BUYER

Marjorie was a compulsive buyer. She belongs in the same general category as Don and Fred, who were also compulsive—though in different ways. Her neurosis simply took another direction. Marjorie bought things simply because they were on sale. Her husband complained to no avail, pointing out that nothing is a bargain if you don't need it. She insisted that the things she bought *would* be needed.

Marjorie was using compulsive buying to handle her deep-seated anxiety. She was not fully aware of this anxiety, and therefore could not resolve it. Buying things allayed her inner tension for the moment, but in a short time the old compulsion was back again as strong as ever.

Marjorie's anxiety dated from childhood. There were some marital tensions, too, but these were simply reinforcing the thirty-year-old buried traumas of childhood, which were the cause of her underlying neurosis.

Arlene was afflicted with obsessive thinking. A thought entered her mind and ran around and around, repetitiously, like a squirrel in a cage. The more she tried to push the idea from her consciousness, the more it dug in. Some of her thoughts were of a sexual nature, while others had to do with self-destruction or self-mutilation. Nothing in her current life situation was sufficiently serious to explain these nonrational thoughts.

In Arlene's case long-term group therapy, plus some individual counseling, helped rid her of nearly all of the obsessive thoughts. Occasionally they returned, but she was able to handle them rather easily. She was taught not to try to force an idea out of her mind, but rather to accept it, and later to replace it gently with another thought or some physical activity. In the process of therapy, she also dealt with her childhood traumas and talked them out.

THE COMPULSIVE LIAR

Henry was a pathological liar. But he was usually unaware of the fact that he was lying. The penalty of liars is that they finally cannot distinguish truth from falsehood and come to believe their own lies. Such people have deep feelings of inferiority and insecurity. This type of neurosis, like others, originates in childhood.

Henry had had an inadequate education, which caused him to feel deficient. He did have lots of drive and considerable ability, and these things gave him a measure of success. But they did not obliterate his inferiority feelings. In an effort to impress people, Henry exaggerated shamelessly. Eventually he began to lie about business matters. His lies finally caught up with him and he ended up bankrupt. A bit later, he was killed in an automobile accident.

INSOMNIA

Francine was an insomniac. It was not unusual for her to go three or four nights with only one or two hours of sleep, then spend twelve hours in a drugged-like condition. In her case there was not one, but several, causes.

Francine's childhood had been seriously marred by fights between her parents, and she had been sexually molested by a neighbor. Primal Integration therapy helped uncover the roots of her faulty sleep pattern. It also revealed that she had a great deal of legitimate anger, which she had difficulty expressing.

Childhood insecurity, traumas, and guilt feelings, coupled with current life situations that produce anxiety, can cause severe insomnia. Some universities have sleep clinics, where the problem is sometimes dealt with successfully. Usually, long-term therapy is indicated.

COMPULSIVE EATERS

Clara was a compulsive eater. She was some eighty-five pounds overweight. Dieting had proved futile in her case, as the roots of her compulsiveness lay far in the past. Food was Clara's tranquilizer; she literally ate in order to keep her anxiety level down. Logic, threats, bribes, and talk therapy had also proved ineffective in Clara's case, for they did not deal with the basic cause of her neurosis.

Several telling things were discovered in Primal Integration therapy. Clara had been sexually molested as a child, which made her fear her sexuality. She came to see that she had gained weight partly in an unconscious effort not to look attractive to men. In addition, she had experienced considerable insecurity as a child. She was now stuffing herself with food as a substitute for love.

THE ALCOHOLIC

Peter was an alcoholic. His wife and four children had lost virtually all respect for him. He made a pretense of going to Alcoholics Anonymous, but only in an effort to impress the judge at the divorce hearing. Like all alcoholics, Peter lied about his drinking. He would state flatly and dogmatically that he had not had a drink when he was obviously drunk.

Peter was a Christian, and one part of his nature fervently wanted the will of God for his life. He had genuine ability and a delightful personality, and he had shown much promise as a young man; but his frantic efforts to "make it big," plus his alcoholism, prevented him from earning a decent living.

Intensive therapy revealed a troubled childhood. There had been an absentee father and an unloving mother. Peter was unconsciously seeking to make his wife a mother substitute and at the same time trying to control her. We encouraged his wife to attend Alanon, the arm of the AA organization that works with family members of an alcoholic.

Unfortunately, pleas and tears had no effect on Peter. He couldn't consider the possibility of facing life without alcohol to deaden his all-pervasive anxiety. His wife eventually divorced him.

Occasionally an alcoholic resolves his or her drinking problem. Allen was one such person.

Allen was married to a charming young wife. He had a splendid position and earned a good income, and they had a lovely home in the suburbs. Then Allen began to drink excessively. Often he would drink for several hours after work, then phone his wife to come and get him in the city. She—patiently, uncomplainingly—scooped him up and drove him home.

Nothing could induce Allen to attend AA. Eventually, when he lost his job and his health was severely threatened, he committed himself to a mental institution. He was there for about six months.

Upon release, Allen had difficulty finding a job. His wife worked to support them. Finally, in desperation, he began to sneak drinks, and before long he was drinking heavily again.

On a sudden impulse I phoned him one day and said, "Allen, I am going to a weekend retreat a hundred miles south of here. Would you care to go with me?" He said, "God must have led you to call. I've been desperate."

Allen seemed to enjoy the weekend, though I had no expectation that the experience by itself would provide the answer he needed. However, he met a delightful woman at the retreat who openly shared the fact that she was a recovered alcoholic. She told him that she was a faithful member of AA, and that it was the only thing that had saved her marriage and her sanity. Allen responded to her enthusiasm and began attending AA meetings with her. He stopped his drinking, and in a matter of months he found another job. In a year or two he had a big promotion and was on his way again.

AA people state categorically that an alcoholic must "hit bottom" before he or she will admit to needing help. This bottom may be the loss of his or her job, family, home, or health—or all of these.

THE TALKAHOLIC

The compulsive talker talks up a storm in order to discharge a load of excess anxiety. As with other forms of neurosis, the origin lies hidden in childhood experiences. Usually there are feelings of insecurity and inferiority, coupled with a moderately to strongly aggressive personality. Just as the problem drinker feels a need to drink in order to face life, the compulsive talker *must* talk to hold the anxiety down. Such a person may not *be* inferior, but *feels* inferior or inadequate.

Occasionally the compulsive talker is also a boaster, leading listeners to comment on what a big ego he has. But it is quite the opposite. The loudmouthed boaster, regardless of his station in life—corporation president or day laborer—has a small ego.

Such people have weak self-esteem. They may have succeeded in some line of work, or even amassed a fortune or titles or degrees, but their aggressive, egocentric stance shouts to the world, "I do not feel adequate; I am insecure despite my achievements. Listen to me, hear me, while I tell you what a great person I am. I need your approval to bolster my ego." They hunger for the spotlight and feel a great sense of loss when they do not have it.

THE DEBATER

Then there is the Debater, who argues each point until—hopefully—others can be forced to agree. This person usually has fragile self-esteem and considerable aggressive drive. If educated, the debater may argue with less vehemence and more polish. If uneducated, he or she will pretend a knowledge of things he or she could not possibly know anything about.

Carl was a fine Christian, upright and compassionate. He loved his family and was kind to friends. But when he differed with someone, he would argue heatedly and endlessly. His education was very limited, and he read very little. He did not have the background and knowledge to present a reasonable argument. Yet he was known to shout, when cornered in an argument, "Don't dispute my word! I know what I'm talking about!"

Carl had a weak self-image. Because of this, he was never known to admit that he could possibly be wrong.

NEVER WRONG

A friend of mine said to me, sadly, "I've been married for forty years. Not once in all that time has my wife ever said, 'I was wrong,' or 'I'm sorry.'"

I said, "My friend, I don't know your wife, but I am sure that she received very little approval and love from her parents. Her self-worth is very low. To admit an error would desolate her. She must always be right or feel a terrible loss of self-esteem. Give her lots of sincere praise and recognition. She needs it desperately."

"What about her never admitting that she is wrong?" he asked.

"Live with it. At her age she is not going to change. Give her as much concern and compassion as if she were a diabetic or had a weak heart."

THE AUTHORITY

Related to the Debater is the Authority. This person seeks to be an authority on virtually everything. He or she may not debate or argue, but will insist on sounding authoritative on anything and everything.

I recall listening in on a conversation in which a woman was informing an Australian acquaintance of certain things about her own country. The speaker had never visited Australia, but she had apparently read a little about its flora and fauna. So she proceeded to tell her amused listener all about it.

The Authority seldom asks questions. To do so would imply a lack of knowledge, and because of a weak ego the Authority must always lecture or inform.

One creative way for the Authority to compensate for the deep sense of insecurity that is at the root of the problem is to become a teacher. This enables the Authority to instruct and inform, thus securing some release from the anxiety. However, it is not a cure.

An Authority with a severe case of insecurity may hesitate to ask directions when searching for an address in an unfamiliar part of the city. If compelled to seek help, he may say, "Now, 185 Chestnut Street is in this general area, right? And I go just a few blocks north to find it."

"No, it's four miles south of here, and you have to go left at the next stoplight."

"Right. That's what I thought."

This sounds so patently ridiculous as to be absurd, but I have known a number of amiable neurotics who went through life like that. Their weak self-image demanded that they remain the all-wise Authority.

ARROGANCE

The arrogant person illustrates a severe neurosis. A cartoon depicts a psychiatrist who says to a new patient, "I'm not aware of your particular problem, so suppose you start at the beginning."

Patient: "All right. In the beginning I created the heavens and the earth."

Arrogance, a manifestation of pride or vanity, is compensation for strong feelings of insecurity. Sometimes it is partially concealed beneath a veneer of intellectuality. This emotional problem may afflict a corporation president, a truck driver, a minister, a salesperson, a homemaker—in a word, persons from any walk of life.

Socrates once listened for a time to an orator at the Agora and finally stopped him with the comment, "I can see your vanity, Antisthenes, through the holes in your cloak." Although he pretended humility, the man's arrogance was still visible in every aspect of his being. Pride is difficult to conceal.

There are varying degrees of pride, vanity, and arrogance. Or it might be more apt to say that these are different aspects of the same neurosis. For instance, the eighty-nine-year-old king of Swaziland, whose country is roughly the size of New Jersey, has given himself these titles in addition to King: The Lion, The Sun, The Milky Way, The Master in Weapons, The Obstacle to the Enemy, The Mouth That Speaks No Lies, The Miraculous Body That Grows Feathers in Winter While Others Are Without Plumage, and The Jaw That Cracks All Bones.

I once had an acquaintance roughly my own age whose undeniably good mind had won him numerous earned and honorary degrees. I had observed him on his own home ground, an expansive, friendly talkative man with a great deal of the Teacher/Authority complex. When he visited me this tendency was exaggerated. Away from his own turf his deep insecurities revealed themselves in compulsive talking and in other ways.

At one point he said expansively, fingertips together, "Now, this morning I had a brilliant thought. I want you to get a piece of paper and a pencil and write this down. You see, when we write things down we tend to remember them longer."

Smiling to myself, I reached for a piece of paper and prepared to jot down the intellectual gem he promised. It was far from earthshaking. I listened to his authoritarian discourse at great length until, overwhelmed and a bit out of patience, I challenged him at some point rather bluntly.

Instantly he crumpled and his voice changed. He sounded contrite and apologetic. My challenging some absurd statement had punctured the balloon of his inflated pride, and he acted for a time like a hurt little boy. I could understand that, for it is in childhood that all of our neurotic behavior patterns originate.

Then there are the abnormally shy persons. Dr. Phillip G. Zimbardo, professor of social psychology at Stanford University and author of four books on the subject of shyness and related personality problems, states that forty percent of all Americans consider themselves shy. That is around eighty-four million people. He says that this includes not only the wallflowers, but a substantial number of celebrities as well.

Among those notables who admit to shyness, surprisingly enough, are people like former President and Mrs. Carter, Prince Charles, Warren Beatty, Catherine Deneuve, and any number of professional athletes. The list also includes people like Carol Burnett, Barbara Walters, and many others who do not give the least impression of shyness.

Dr. Zimbardo's research indicates that the basic cause of shyness appears to be the relationships we have had with other people, either in childhood or later. But some people who were very shy as children overcome it and do not consider themselves to be shy as adults.

There are people so timid that they do not even go to pick up their unemployment checks. A lesser degree of shyness prevents some sufferers from asking questions. One highly successful man who does not give the slightest impression of being shy tells me that in a supermarket he has to force himself to ask a stock boy where some article can be found.

Shy people imagine that others are constantly evaluating their performance, whether it is playing golf, walking down the aisle at church, or mowing the lawn. They are usually very self-conscious. A delightful woman of fifty told me that she had walked a certain business street every day for three weeks, yet hadn't the slightest idea what the town looked like because she always walked with her eyes downcast.

Such self-consciousness does not originate in vanity, but in a fear of judgment, condemnation, or criticism. Judgmental or critical parents, feelings of rejection in childhood, and fear of being judged guilty or wrong, are usually at the root of shyness. Sometimes it is intensified by the example of a timid, fearful parent.

One may attain significant goals and be considered highly successful, yet have an underlying shyness. Some aggressive people hide their shyness behind a gruff manner, while others maintain a cold, aloof facade. The more passive ones tend to withdraw from social contact as much as possible.

Conquering shyness is not simple. There are several basic principles, however, that are fundamental to doing this.

The first is William James's "act as if" principle: Do the thing you fear to do, and in time your feelings will catch up with your emotions. It works like this:

A timid person maps out a program whereby he or she reaches out to someone. The first step is to introduce himself/herself to a stranger at church or in a social setting. The next step after the introduction is to ask appropriate questions. A list of such questions should be thought out in advance and memorized. Talking about the other person takes the spotlight from the shy person and thus reduces self-consciousness.

In some cases a competent counselor—psychologist or psychiatrist—can be of help in outlining such a program.

In relating to shy persons, one should never refer to their disability. "You're quite shy, aren't you?" is on a par with saying to an exceedingly homely person, "You're really pretty ugly, aren't you?"

Quite often a timid person is married to a much more outgoing mate. Usually the more extroverted one does most of the talking. This is all right if it is mutually agreeable to both; but if a friendly, outgoing spouse breezes ahead in every situation, leaving the other in the shadows, this can pose a problem.

PROCRASTINATORS

Procrastinators comprise a special category. They may be normal in every other respect, yet go through life manufacturing excuses for being late and doing on Thursday what had been promised on Monday. Procrastination is a personality defect that is not readily resolved, certainly not by recrimination. Criticism, rewards, punishment, are all unavailing.

Some of these persons were overcoerced as children, and the only way they could win was by rebelling. Instead of open defiance, they learned to rebel against pressure by procrastinating.

Others seem to have developed the trait due to a lack of discipline. Not having had to do things at any specific time; never having learned to do what they should do, when they should do it, whether they liked it or not, they developed the habit of postponing things and took the path of least resistance. Still others seem to acquire this tendency by osmosis—that is, by following the example of a parent or an older sibling.

The procrastinator suffers to some extent, but usually not as much as his or her associates or family. Living with such a person can be exasperating. Sometimes a quiet, good-natured procrastinator is married to a dynamic personality who is well organized. If both are reasonably satisfied, then it is a fine symbiotic relationship. Usually, however, it poses severe problems. The spouse who never pays the bills until they are long overdue, or who is so disorganized that laundry is stacked up all over the house, can find reasons for his or her habitual delays; but living with these foot-draggers can be tremendously irritating. As a general rule, only deep therapy will resolve the problem.

Everyone is familiar with the noble exhortation, "Never put off until tomorrow what you can do today," but few are aware that the author of that bit of wisdom was the elegant Lord Chesterfield, one of the great procrastinators of all time. He never got around to marrying his son's mother, and he had a habit of keeping dignitaries cooling their heels in the waiting room. His oft-quoted adage about not putting things off was no doubt a short-term effort to exorcise his own demon of procrastination.

One Roman general was dubbed "Cuntator" ("Delayer") because he was forever putting off battles until the last possible moment.

In many instances the delaying tactics are an effort to avoid making decisions. If a child was punished or criticized for making mistakes, one solution was to postpone making any decision as long as possible to avoid the feared parental response. This is a totally unconscious reaction, of course.

JEALOUSY AND POSSESSIVENESS

Almost everyone is capable of jealousy to some degree. A person who exhibits intense jealousy is to that degree neurotic, and correspondingly miserable. Jealousy and possessiveness often go hand in hand. As with other neurotic tendencies, their origins are in the past. The insecurity, dependency, and inferiority at the root of jealousy can cause a person to act in an unreasonable or even bizarre manner.

One man was so possessive and jealous of his wife that he would not permit her to go to the supermarket alone, lest she flirt with the checker. He listened in on her telephone conversations and demanded to know to whom she was talking. He felt abandoned if she was not at his side more or less constantly. In Primal Integration therapy he relived the pain he felt at age three when his mother died.

A woman quizzed her husband intensively whenever he came home from a business trip. She asked persistently about his actions each evening that he had been away. The inquisition usually took place at dinner the first night he was home. He told me, "I have come to hate those interrogations. She quietly but insistently needs to know everything I did on a given evening. Good heavens, I have to rack my mind to try to reconstruct my schedule. I've never been unfaithful to my wife, and I don't intend to be, but if she keeps up this insane jealousy, I just don't know. . . ."

A discussion with this woman revealed the fact that her parents had divorced when she was quite small. Daddy had left: "went away" was her phrase. So she had a deep, nonlogical fear that her husband might "go away," too. The child within was still there.

No amount of logic or reasoning will diminish jealousy. The conscious mind has no direct control over such emotions.

People who are quite normal in every other respect can be made to feel insecure, jealous, or deeply hurt under certain conditions. One man shared with me a painful lesson he had learned in this regard.

"I share everything with my wife," he told me. "When I tell her about a man whom I admire, that is all right, of course; but once, when I made the mistake of praising a very pretty woman a few years younger than she, she was silent for three days. I could see that she was hurt. She would never admit to being a jealous person, but I learned never to praise another woman in her presence. That's her sore point." While this does not constitute a severe neurotic tendency, it would have to be categorized as jealousy originating in insecurity.

We can get along better with people if we understand *why* they act as they do. Here is a short list of some defenses commonly used to mask neuroses:

Repression is a process whereby threatening thoughts or feelings or actions are buried deep in the unconscious. They are "forgotten," but they can be dredged up and reexperienced.

Denial is a very widely used defense. When a thought or feeling seems unacceptable, a person uses denial to repudiate the threatening thought or feeling and thus to avoid anxiety.

Projection is another unconscious process whereby one can disown unacceptable thoughts, ideas, or motives. To achieve this it becomes necessary to attribute these ideas or feelings to another person: "It is not I who hate you; it is you who hate me."

Projection operates in the daily lives of most people at one time or another. An office manager described an employee who, on occasion, would begin to shout angrily over trifles. When reprimanded and told to "stop screaming," he would shout in reply, "*I'm* not screaming, *you* are, and I won't take it any longer." He sincerely believed that he was not shouting.

Rationalization is another interesting mechanism that is utilized by almost everyone at times. We react on the basis of our emotions, then whip up a handy, reasonable-sounding explanation for our action. This prevents us from feeling the anxiety resulting from a lowered self-esteem. We can't think highly of ourselves unless we seem to act rationally.

Failure can be rationalized:

"I didn't have time to finish the job."

"I was interrupted or I'd have gotten it done."

"I have done all the work on my Ph.D.—that is, except for the thesis. I've been too busy to get started on it."

"People (meaning oneself) wouldn't cheat on their income taxes if politicians weren't all crooked."

Sexual promiscuity can be rationalized with the excuse that "We're sexually liberated. Everyone does it."

Reaction Formation is an unconscious defense against anxiety. When we have an attitude or feeling that is too threatening, we adopt precisely the *opposite* attitude and claim it for our own.

A young woman was struggling with a powerful attraction for a handsome young man. He showed no interest in her whatever. When she realized that her feelings would not be reciprocated, she announced to her friends that she simply couldn't stand him: "He's the most conceited man I've ever met. I wouldn't date him if he were the last man on earth. I despise him." She managed to convince herself that this was true, even if no one else believed it.

Displacement is another way of handling anxiety. A man is chewed out by his boss. It isn't wise to tell him off, so he holds his anger in until he gets home. At dinner he blows up over the way the meat is cooked. His wife later snaps at one of the older children, who in turn slaps his little brother for some fancied wrong. The smaller child then kicks the cat. Hence the term "catkicking."

Insecure people with inferiority feelings often displace their self-hate onto minority groups. A woman who was terrorized by her father may take out her anger on her husband. The school bully who cannot express his rage at his parents may displace his frustration onto smaller children. And so on.

Regression is a retreat from adult behavior to earlier childlike conduct in an effort to avoid facing some unpleasant situation. Some children, feeling insecure, will regress to infantile behavior in an unconscious effort to get the unconditional love received as an infant. An older child under stress may regress to thumb sucking. Adults escape the tension of daily life by playing games, throwing snowballs, and engaging in horseplay—in short, by acting like children again. This called "regression in the service of the ego." It is harmless and provides momentary release from tension.

Compensation is an unconscious process whereby one may conceal some weakness or deficiency by emphasizing a more desirable aspect of the personality. One may compensate for feelings of inadequacy by learning to excel in some area. Alfred Adler, who coined the term "inferiority complex," compensated for his lack of social aptitude by making good grades in school. This can be a helpful device when used appropriately.

Intellectualization is an unconscious mechanism whereby we protect ourselves from feeling the full impact of our emotions. By analyzing a situation and using our intellectual powers, we defend ourselves against feelings. The school system emphasizes scholastic aptitude at the expense of emotional development. A majority of educated people fear their emotions and use this device quite consistently. The loss of spontaneity is the price they pay for this.

Phobias serve to protect one from threatening situations, thoughts, or feelings. A phobia is simply an irrational fear. A man with a handwashing compulsion and a crippling fear of contamination discovered in therapy that his phobia originated in a sexual encounter over which he felt great guilt. He then was led to see that his irrational fear had deeper roots extending back to infancy. He had been a sickly child and was overprotected by his mother, who had a monumental fear of germs.

There are scores of phobias, with a dozen or two being the most common. It is worse than futile to try to talk someone out of any irrational fear.

Each of the aforementioned mechanisms is a defense against some real or imagined threat to the self. Laughter, crying, swearing, smoking, drinking, TV watching, overtalking, compulsive working or socializing, could all be considered defenses. Some are more acceptable than others, and serve us well. Others can be destructive.

When we understand why people act as they do, we can relate to them more effectively. And when we realize that all of us are to some degree neurotic, we can sense more deeply why Jesus urged us to "Judge not, lest you be judged."

Go very gently today, for everyone you will
meet is carrying an almost intolerable bur-
den.   —*Michelle Flaubert*

7 • Getting Along With Difficult People

The only thing I recall learning in the fourth grade was one of Aesop's fables.

It seems that the sun and the wind had an argument as to which of them was the stronger. The wind spoke of the power of his hurricanes, while the sun alluded to his strength in lifting water from the oceans and lakes. The argument was going nowhere until they spotted a man walking along a road wearing a heavy coat.

The sun challenged the wind to make the man take off his coat. So the wind blew up a gale, but the man only clutched his coat more firmly about him. The sun then said, "Let me try." He came out from behind a cloud and bore down with quiet intensity. In a few moments the man took off his coat and threw it across his arm. Thus, proclaimed Aesop, was the superior power of the quiet sun demonstrated.

I haven't read the story since I was nine years old. But as I recall it, the essence of this simple fable is that quiet strength can often outperform loud bluster.

A young woman once came to see me to discuss religion. Announcing that she was an ardent Roman Catholic, she proceeded to challenge some fairly well established Protestant beliefs. I look back on that encounter with considerable embarrassment, for it was an exercise in futility. Not realizing that she had not really come to challenge my religious views, but because she was uncertain about her own, I let myself be drawn into a foolish argument.

At first I was reasonably tactful and drew her out. A bit later, as she challenged some of my beliefs, I found myself growing defensive. I began to debate with her—a genuinely irrational approach. After half an hour of fruitless argument she arose and with considerable heat declared, "I'm more convinced than ever that we Catholics are right!"

My great error was in bothering to defend the Protestant position. It needed no more defense than her Catholic theology did. I should have asked the young woman to explain to me things about her faith that I did not fully understand. In time, I am convinced, she would have shared the areas of her religious uncertainty and confusion. Then I could have focused on our areas of common belief. Being much younger then, however, I lacked some of the common sense that comes with experience and age.

A head-on argument seldom solves anything. And sometimes it can be disastrous.

A RELUCTANT SELLER

We once wanted to purchase several houses across the street from our church. The first owner posed no problem, nor did the second. But the third one did. The retired man who owned the property was a dedicated pack rat. When I asked if he would consider selling his house, he took me to the basement and showed me an amazing assortment of miscellaneous items he had acquired through fifty years of shopping for bargains. There were dozens of plumbing fixtures, most in poor condition; used furniture he had picked up at sales, and forty different varieties of what appeared to be pure junk. To him it was a priceless collection. "If I were to move," he said, "I'd have to move all my valuable things, and it would cost a small fortune. We've thought of moving to a smaller house, but I'm not in good health, and it makes me tired just to think about moving all those things." I said I could sympathize with him, because I, too, was a collector.

A few weeks later I chanced to see this man in his front yard pruning some rose bushes. I said, "My friend, I've been thinking about that collection you have in your basement; I may have a solution."

"Yes, what is it?"

"I've talked to my board, and they have agreed to hire half a dozen men and the biggest moving van in the city to move your collection—at no expense to you."

His face lit up. Then he seized my hand and shook it vigorously. "You'd do that for me? Why, I think that's wonderful. I'll go and tell Sarah; she's been wanting to move, and this will really please her."

A few days later he came to tell me that they would be glad to accept our offer. Three months later when they moved, his wife convinced him that there wouldn't be room at the new home for his priceless "collection." They left it in the basement, and we paid $150 to have it hauled to the dump. Patience and the "soft sell" often work best.

POOR SALESMANSHIP

You may have had the experience of having someone try to sell you something you didn't want, or convert you to some new religion or ideology, or change your mind. It made you either irritated or angry, didn't it? It is poor salesmanship and wretched human relations for people to try to force you to accept their merchandise, their ideas, or anything else you don't particularly want.

Some years ago I was on the verge of buying a new car. The salesman and I had agreed on the price, and he had started writing up the order. Suddenly he stopped and said, "I guess I'd better check this out with the sales manager. I'll be right back." He returned in a few minutes with his boss, who explained that the salesman had been overly generous. They'd have to charge me $300 more.

The two of them were a bit too oily, too smooth, too quietly insistent, too persuasive. It was obvious that they were using an old sales trick. I had found the car I wanted, with just the right accessories. I had driven it, and I liked it. I had already spent several hours in the salesroom and had made out my check. I was sold, and they knew it. So they sprang the trap.

"I'm sorry," I said, "but I don't appreciate your methods. Hand me back my check, because I am not going to buy this car at any price."

Then began the sales pitch, the frantic arguments; but I got my check back, tore it up, and left.

The next morning the salesman was in my office, trying again. They found that they could meet my offer after all, he said.

"No, I'm sorry," I told him. "I will buy my car from another agency. I feel insulted by your sales tactics."

He seemed amazed. After all, it usually worked; what had gone wrong?

I have a friend who is a real estate broker. He may never get rich, but he will always have my respect and admiration. He is very low-key, and he doesn't try to "sell" a house or business. If it is to be an investment, he first wants to know your general tax bracket, how long you want to keep the property, and a dozen other things. Then he spends considerable time with his adding machine. Finally he comes up with a page or two of figures. He may point out that, in your particular tax bracket, it would not be a good investment for you. In that case he asks for more time to find something that will suit your purposes better. He never pushes, never argues.

What a pleasure it is to do business with a person like that! I think he probably sleeps well at night, for he has an easy conscience. Everyone admires him.

As a student, I once taught night school, preparing foreigners for their citizenship examination by a federal examiner. Most of the students were people of humble origin. All who had taken my course had been passed by the examiner.

At one hearing in the federal building a very haughty woman dripping with diamonds appeared along with my students and was questioned by the examiner. She was a very wealthy Canadian who had disdained attending my classes because the people were "not on her social level," as she told him. Because the woman could answer none of his questions about the United States and its form of government, the examiner refused to pass her. She was very indignant. In a semihysterical rage she declared that she had vast influence and would get him fired.

When everyone had left, the examiner said to me, "She will either have to attend your classes or receive private instruction. If she sees you privately, I want you to charge her $50 an hour."

I phoned the woman a day or two later and offered to give her private instruction, adding that I could guarantee that she would pass. She agreed to meet me in the dorm lounge.

Once a week for three months, she arrived at my dormitory in her chauffeur-driven Rolls-Royce. I spent two hours with her at each session. We both had a good thing: I needed the money and she needed to become an American citizen.

She was sharp—and very determined not to fail her next examination. In fact, she learned so rapidly that I had to work hard to find things for her to memorize. I taught her civics as though she were going up for final exams in a college course. She learned five or six times as much as any applicant for citizenship was required to know.

On the day of examination, the examiner summoned her and asked gently, "Did you receive private instruction?"

"Yes. I studied very hard." The examiner glanced at me, smiling.

"Fine, now tell me about yourself and about Canada."

For fifteen minutes he listened raptly as she talked about her own country. Then, with an enigmatic smile, he said, "I'm sure you know all that is required of a United States citizen, so you can now be sworn in." He asked her not one single question about American history or civics. She looked at him with blank indignation, then wrote out her check and handed it to me.

The woman became a citizen, I got my money, and the examiner had his quiet revenge. He had made her work hard, with my willing connivance, and then had not allowed her to display her newly acquired knowledge of U.S. civics. But was it revenge? Perhaps he simply taught her a valuable lesson: that you do not with impunity threaten a federal officer.

GRUDGES TEND TO BACKFIRE

Getting even is not a particularly worthwhile endeavor. It involves holding a grudge, and a grudge is simply "congealed hatred turned rancid." One's energy is best spent in other ways.

Jim would have denied that he held a grudge against his mother. She had been only fifteen when he was born, an unwanted child, and she had treated him abominably. When he was about nine years old, Jim had determined that he would make it on his own, and he had. He had become a remarkably successful businessman and a delightful person. But his infrequent contacts with his mother always ended disastrously. "She's crazy," he said, without rancor. "I can't even stand to have a telephone conversation with her."

In a series of Primal Integration sessions Jim relived some of his tragic childhood. Much of it had to do with things he had completely forgotten. He was three years old, then four, then five, then seven and eight. In the process of reliving various events, he expressed his hurt, then his fear, and finally his anger—legitimate, violent anger that he didn't know he had.

Toward the end, Jim forgave his mother. He thought he had done this before, but it had been at an intellectual level. Now he forgave her from the bottom of his emotional nature. Later he said, "I still don't want to be around her. I know what I'll do: I'll send her and my stepfather plane tickets and pay their way for two weeks in Hawaii."

The ancient wounds were healed at last, the anger dissipated. Jim felt no affection for his mother, only *agape* love. He had fulfilled Jesus' injunction, "Love your enemies and pray for those who mistreat you."[1]

THEIR DISASTER AND MY HEADACHE

It sounds terribly egocentric, but the truth is that my headache is more real to me than is a terrible tragedy in some distant country. That backache or sinus problem that ails you from time to time probably bothers you more than the knowledge that a hundred thousand homeless people sleep in the streets of Calcutta every night, or that half the world's population will go to bed hungry tonight.

This does not mean that we are heartless, only that it is human nature to be more concerned about ourselves and our problems than those of other people.

Therefore, when you stop focusing on yourself and give sincere attention to someone else, you have done something truly significant for that person. Some people find this very difficult to do.

A minister whom I had not seen for ten years or more dropped in to see me one day. He was all excited, having just returned from the Holy Land.

"Osborne, you must go to the Holy Land! It will be the high point of your life. By all means plan to make the trip." He spent another forty-five minutes eloquently insisting that it would change my life.

I glanced around my office. It was filled—cluttered, really—with artifacts I had brought back with me from eight different trips to the Holy Land. There were forty pieces of ancient glassware, dating from 100 B.C. to A.D. 200; pottery ranging in age from 2,000 B.C. to A.D. 50, and assorted artifacts from some of the sixty-odd other countries I have visited.

But my friend didn't see any of that. He wasn't there in my office; he was in the Holy Land, or in his own private world. I didn't want to spoil his day by telling him how many times I had visited the Holy Land, so I listened while he told me all about the sacred spots he had visited. He was so egocentric that he was aware only of himself.

If you want to get along well with people, *don't burst their bubble.* Don't show them where they are wrong or engage in one-upmanship. Just listen appreciatively.

TEASING AND RIDICULE

A young woman told me that her father had loved to tease her when she was a child. One of his favorite tricks had been to hold out both closed hands. "If you can guess which hand it's in, you can have it," he would say.

"But I never guessed the right hand," she said. "Only after he had done it hundreds of times did I realize that he had nothing in either hand; he was only teasing in a sadistic way. I learned never to believe him, then to mistrust him, and now I despise him."

Teasing can be very painful to a child. Sarcasm falls into the same category, as does ridicule. A child should never be ridiculed—nor, for that matter, should a person of any age.

Ridicule and sarcasm are both disguised hostility. "But I was only joking; can't you take a joke?" is the typical response of the person who employs ridicule under the guise of humor. Insult is added to injury by the insinuation that you are hypersensitive and have no sense of humor.

HOW TO PROVE YOUR SUPERIORITY

You can prove your superiority by never trying to demonstrate it. There is nothing wrong with winning, but there is definitely something wrong with trying to prove your superiority by having to win constantly.

Harold, a friend who often invited me to his home loved games of all sorts: badminton, quoits, darts, and half a dozen others. He enjoyed playing these every Saturday afternoon. One day I played badminton with him and lost. Chuckling, he brought out his darts. I lost again. Then we played three or four other games at which he was quite adept. Finally he asked me to try Ping-Pong. It happened to be one of the few games at which I am rather proficient. I let him have one point in the first game by being generous. At this he stopped chuckling and put away the equipment.

Harold was a poor loser. He never trotted out his Ping-Pong equipment again; we had to play only the games at which he was good. Because I didn't particularly mind losing, he loved playing with me.

THERE ARE NO GOOD LOSERS

It has been said that there are no good losers, only good actors. There is a grain of truth in that, but some people display their weak self-esteem in their aversion to losing. Whether it be a game or a conversation, *don't feel you have to win.* Win the relationship, not the encounter or the game. Take the long-range view; prove your superiority by refusing to demonstrate it.

WIN THE ARGUMENT, LOSE A FRIEND

Hubert was the president of a national corporation. He had a brilliant mind, but poor relationships. One evening at a dinner party in our home, he engaged another corporation president and two topflight executives in a furious argument. The other men rebutted his ridiculous argument mildly, then finally refused to discuss the matter further.

Hubert's wife was overwhelmed with embarrassment. Some time later she told me that she had finally resolved never to accept social engagements with her husband, because he always made all of the other guests angry and ruined the evening for her.

What is the point of succeeding financially if you can't succeed at anything else? Hubert had no real friendships, and his marriage was a shambles. He was rich and unhappy.

HARMLESS AND DESTRUCTIVE WAYS OF COMPENSATING

The poor loser, the argumentative type, the loud-mouth, and the compulsive talker are all trying to compensate for deep feelings of inferiority. But there are relatively harmless ways of compensating for childhood hurts.

While visiting a man in his office, I commented on three teddy bears lined up on his desk. My friend laughed and said, "Those are recent gifts to my collection. I have thirty-two of them at home."

I asked, "Do you want to tell me about it?" He laughed again.

"Sure, I know why I collect them. When I was a kid it was the only toy I was ever given. My parents didn't believe in toys, but they broke over this once and gave me a teddy bear. They were religious fanatics and didn't even believe in observing Christmas, but they made one minor exception. Each Christmas they would take my teddy bear, clean and repair it, wrap it up, and give it to me as a Christmas gift. There was no Christmas tree, of course, and no other gifts. But now I can have all the teddy bears I want. I am compensating for my childhood deprivation." Though he laughed, the memory of his deprived childhood showed behind his laugh.

Later in the day this man drove me to the airport in a Cadillac. I commented on his new acquisition. He said, "Oh, I have two of them, as well as a third car, a smaller one." I looked at him questioningly.

"Sure. I'm compensating again. My father didn't believe in complimenting me. He was afraid I'd become conceited. But when I was seventeen I bought a second-hand Cord, one of the most beautiful cars ever made. I took Dad for a ride in it and got it up to ninety miles an hour. Later I heard him say to my mother, "The kid's got a fine car and he took me for a great ride." That was the only praise, if you can call it that, that I ever got from him."

"So, you're still buying cars hoping to win some approval?"

"Something like that; but as long as I know why I'm doing it and can afford it, it seems O.K. to me." Again he laughed. He was laughing at the manifest absurdity of it, enjoying the little joke on himself, and appreciating his ability to make up now in adulthood for some of his childhood deprivation.

FIFTY-TWO CREDIT CARDS

At the airport, while we were having some coffee, an acquaintance of this man happened to open her purse. He said, "Show him your credit cards." Whereupon she opened up several plastic credit card cases and spread them out for me. I counted fifty-two. They both laughed, and I said, "All right, there is a story behind this, too. Tell me about it." It was brief, but significant.

She had grown up in abject poverty. Her father had only been able to express love in monetary terms. "So, money equals love," she said. "I had to spend all I earned as a kid to help Mom and Dad. So now I have these fifty-two credit cards, a checkbook, and some cash I carry around. Besides, I put a dollar or two aside every day in a special fund. It cannot be spent, though I can borrow from it. This way I have a great feeling of financial security that I didn't have as a child. I know precisely why I have all these symbols of financial security."

If you know that you are compensating for some ancient childhood deprivation and can smile at yourself, such compensation can be a relatively harmless psychological device, provided it doesn't hurt others or interfere significantly with your own life.

THE IN-LAW PROBLEM

Relationships with in-laws come in all shapes, sizes, and intensities. Often there are complications within complications.

Dr. Wayne W. Dyer writes,

At a recent lecture I asked all 800 people in the audience to list the five most common situations in which they felt victimized. *Eighty-three percent* were connected with the victims' families. Imagine, something like 83 percent of your victimization may be due to your ineffectiveness in dealing with family members who end up controlling or manipulating you. And you must be doing the same to them.

Typical family coercions cited were: being forced to visit relatives, to make phone calls, to chauffeur people around, to suffer nagging parents, children, in-laws, angry relatives, to pick up after everyone, generally to be a servant, not to be respected or appreciated by other family members, to spend time with ingrates, to have no privacy because of family expectations, and so on and on.[2]

Gertrude, the youngest of six children, and at thirty-nine still unmarried, had chosen to take care of her aging mother. The other sons and daughters were married and had children of their own, so it seemed the logical thing for her to do. But at forty-one Gertrude decided to marry. Mother, now in poor health and quite elderly, felt threatened by the turn of events. She began to complain of vague but persistent ailments.

Gertrude appealed to her brothers and sisters, asking if they would mind taking mother for at least a few months. They replied with various excuses: they were short of room; there were financial problems; Gertrude had no children as yet and was best able to care for mother. The discussion went on for weeks, in person and by mail. Gertrude's brothers and sisters presented a united front: it was her responsibility because she was youngest and had no children.

Gertrude buried her resentment and went on with the wedding plans. Mother refused to attend the wedding, insisting that she was not feeling well. Two sisters attended the wedding, chiefly because they had been asked to be bridesmaids. Relationships were strained.

Gertrude, her mother, and her new husband, Jack, settled down together in a small house, and for a time mother made a fairly valiant effort to be civil. But within a month or so she grew critical and began retiring to her room immediately after dinner. She also ate her other meals in her room. Jack began to feel uncomfortable, and

Gertrude was becoming depressed from trying to bury her anger.

Jack eventually suggested gently that she call a family conference to see what could be done. Four of her brothers and sisters, and their spouses, elected not to attend. Gertrude then announced that she intended to put her mother in a retirement home.

There was instant recrimination from everyone: "How can you do this to our mother? She'd die in a month in one of those places. After all she's done for you! Of course, *we* can't take her, for reasons you clearly understand; but you, with no children, surely ought to be able to take care of her until the end . . ." and on and on and on.

Gertrude began to feel guilt on top of her buried anger. Increasingly depressed, she sought counseling.

After hearing the story, the counselor asked, "What are your options?" She could think of none. He pointed out several.

She could let the situation remain as it was and live in her depressed state. Under those circumstances, there was always the possibility that her husband might lose interest and leave her.

Or she could try to reason with her brothers and sisters. "No, that's out," she explained. "They're hopeless. I want nothing to do with them."

The third alternative was putting her mother in a retirement home. "But they'll all hate me," objected Gertrude.

"Do they love you now?"

"They say they do, but—"

"But what?"

"They don't act like it."

"What do you want: peace of mind and a viable solution, or to hang onto the illusion that your brothers and sisters really care about you?"

The session lasted another half-hour. Gertrude finally elected to put her mother in a retirement home.

When her mother heard the news, she protested that she wasn't going. Brothers and sisters and their mates protested that she couldn't do this to their mother. But Gertrude was adamant.

Mother was put in a retirement home. In a few months she was feeling much better, running the recreation program and giving devotionals for the women's Bible class with sufficient energy left over to make life fairly miserable for the staff. When told that she would have to stop stirring things up with her gossip and complaints or leave, she became quite tractable and began to enjoy her new life.

Gertrude and Jack still have impaired relations with her brothers and sisters. But she has learned that it is their problem. She came to see that their resentment stemmed chiefly from their own guilt.

There may never be a happy solution for these impaired relationships. Gertrude treats her siblings politely, refuses to argue, and sends Christmas cards annually. She says, "You can pick your friends, but you inherit your relatives. The door is open if they ever want to make gestures of reconciliation. If they do, it would be wonderful. If not, it isn't fatal. I am happy in my marriage, and life is good."

It would be nice if there could always be a happy ending to every story, as in the books and movies. But life isn't like that. Sometimes there *is* no perfect solution, and we have to do the best we can and be satisfied with that.

A man driving through a rural area of West Virginia paused to ask directions of a boy in overalls seated on a fence. The motorist asked, "Have you lived here all your life?"

The boy chewed on a blade of grass for a moment, then said solemnly, "No, just 'til now."

You have the rest of your life in which to resolve your problems and to achieve some of your goals. Give it your best, and don't worry about the rest.

The tiger does not declare his "tigritude" before he pounces. He declares it in the elegance of his leap.

—*Wolfe Soyinka,*
Nigerian dramatist

8 • When and How to Confront

A physician friend of mine purchased an expensive new car. The first week he had it, it developed a serious malfunction, so he took it back to the dealer for repairs. Two weeks later there was more trouble. Over the next three months he had it in the garage four more times.

One day the brakes failed while his wife was driving the car. She avoided an accident only by providence and quick reflexes. My friend asked the dealer to send a tow truck for the car and complained strongly about the situation. The dealer did not seem disturbed, but agreed to try to fix the faulty braking system. The third day after it had been repaired, the brakes failed again.

This time my friend phoned the executive vice president in charge of sales in Detroit. In clear, cold, measured tones he described his experience with the car. Then he said, "At the moment, the car seems to be running satisfactorily, having been patched up several times by the rather indifferent dealer. But I want you to know that if I or any member of my family is injured due to the malfunctioning of this car, I will immediately sue your company for a million dollars."

The vice president was alarmed. "Doctor, listen, don't drive that car! I repeat, *do not drive that car*. Rent a car and send the bill to us. I will have a new car for you within a week. But remember, don't drive the car!"

Why did my friend get results? First, he did the appropriate thing in complaining to the owner of the dealership, rather than to a mechanic, each time the car malfunctioned. Second, he didn't get angry or shout, or make demands. But when it was apparent that the car he had bought was a lemon, and that the local dealer was not going to remedy the situation, he took concrete action and went directly to the top.

When it comes to confrontation, people fall into five general categories:

1. *The Accusers*

These people are great faultfinders and critics, refusing to accept any blame themselves. They tend to play the game of uproar, and others scatter to avoid their angry accusations. However, if firmly challenged, they often crumple after putting up token resistance.

2. *The Placators*

The Placators will do virtually anything to avoid a confrontation. They apologize for living, and cringe before the slightest hint of criticism. They are ingratiating and have a strong need to win approval from everyone. Such people cannot endure rejection and will go to any lengths to avoid it.

3. *The Instructors*

These persons have a strong need to inform and to teach and are great intellectualizers. Being out of touch with their deeper emotions, they are insensitive to the feelings of others. They are proud of the ability to "rise above" emotions and are all head and no heart.

4. *The Diverters*

Such people have a policy of confusing the issue. They employ diversions to avoid a direct confrontation. Very often they use a rush of words to becloud the issue, hoping it will go away.

5. *The Levelers*

These people are open and direct and face an issue directly without becoming angry. They are succinct and logical, use tact, and are considerate of the feelings of others. They do not accuse, but simply state the facts as they see them.

Many people will do almost anything to avoid a confrontation. They have such a great need to be liked that a face-to-face encounter becomes a traumatic situation.

THE ANGRY CONFRONTER

There is an interesting reason why some people become angry and shout during a confrontation. The Placators, who genuinely fear a confrontation, see only two options: retreat or attack. Normally these people retreat, but when fear or frustration overwhelms them, they feel a need to confront. They cannot do this until they get very angry. Fearing their opponent and the opponent's anger, they may become inappropriately angry.

A very amiable woman who worked for me stalked into my office one day and began to shout at me. She made all manner of accusations about being treated unfairly, complained of not having received a raise, and told me loudly that she didn't intend to put up with it.

When she finally subsided a bit, I said, "I think much of what you have to say has merit. I'll be glad to discuss it with you. But can you tell me why you are so angry?"

She thought for a moment, still breathing hard, and finally said, rather meekly, "I think my problem is that I couldn't just come in here and ask you for a raise until I got good and mad. I've been getting this anger up for three whole days, and now you've burst my bubble by agreeing with me." She laughed.

I said, "Yes, I've been thinking about the matter of a raise for you, because you deserve one."

She said, "Thanks, and I'm sorry I got so mad. I'm not mad at you, just at myself for being so scared."

If you have a complaint about the way you have been treated by a business firm, don't take it to a clerk. The salesperson usually has little interest in whether you are pleased or displeased. *Take your complaint to the top.* This may be the department head, the sales manager, or the vice president. In the case of a smaller firm, you may need to make an appointment with the owner.

Don't storm in and make a lot of accusations. State the problem calmly. Have your sales slip or other documentation with you. Prepare a written list of your complaints.

Don't threaten to take your business elsewhere. While the owner or official doesn't want to lose a customer and would prefer to have your goodwill, your threat doesn't carry a great deal of weight. Besides, threats put him or her on the defensive.

In California, as in some other states, there is a Department of Consumer Affairs. As a last resort, when negotiations fail, dissatisfied customers write to the department, stating the pertinent facts. However, it is always best to try to work things out first with the department head or whoever is ultimately responsible.

Whether you have been mistreated by a firm or an individual, there are certain words best avoided, such as "should" and "ought." Telling an adult what he ought to do seldom contributes anything helpful to a satisfactory relationship.

IT IS FUTILE TO TRY TO CHANGE PEOPLE

Only God knows how many husbands and wives have wasted untold hours and years trying to change each other.

In a counseling session a woman told me, with unconcealed bitterness, of her thirty-five-year struggle to change her husband. "He's hopeless," she complained. "You met him; you saw how weak and spineless he is. I have to do everything. He's a rotten father and a lousy husband. I want a divorce."

The husband *was* rather passive, and it was obvious that he had unconsciously married a strong mother figure. But I sensed that he was much less a man than he had been earlier. Thirty-five years of hostile criticism had left him emotionally paralyzed. He wanted to escape from her angry outbursts as much as she wanted to be free of an ineffectual husband. Their problem was resolved only after extensive counseling, when she agreed to cease her critical attacks and he learned to treat her as a wife rather than as the dominant mother he had feared as a child.

It seems evident to us that a great many people need to be changed. Some of them seem pretty weird, don't they? But you are wasting your time trying to change them. Basic changes in an adult's personality cannot be brought about until that person *wants* to change; and your efforts to get him or her to change will usually make him or her angry—a counterproductive approach.

It is impossible for you to change
—a timid person into an outgoing one.
—an intellectualizer into a genuinely feeling person.
—a compulsive talker into a quiet, reflective type of individual.
—a cautious individual into a daring, venturesome one.
—an impetuous person into a cautious or careful one.
—a spendthrift into a miser.
—a pinchpenny into an openhanded, generous individual.

Such persons may change, but not as a result of your advice or criticism. You cannot get other people to feel as you do—to have your identical moods, ideas, concerns, and attitudes.

How Our Personalities Develop

Think of the incredible number of complex factors that go into the formation of a personality. First there is the matter of genetic makeup. In the act of intercourse that precedes conception, several million sperm are released, each with a different DNA molecule carrying the code for physical, mental, and emotional traits. Only one of the sperm will reach the egg. After fertilization there is a combination of DNA molecules carrying many bits of coded information that will predispose the child to be tall or short, shy or aggressive, brown-eyed or blue-eyed, and so on. Literally hundreds of other traits are genetically predetermined.

During the nine-month gestation period, the mother's physical and emotional state has a bearing on the unborn infant. What she feels is transmitted to the fetus. The medication she takes, the balance of minerals and vitamins in the food she eats, all affect it.

Then there is the matter of birth—one of the most traumatic events this new life will ever go through. For some it is a terrible experience; for others, simply a frightening episode as they leave the warmth and safety of the womb to emerge cold, hungry, and frightened in a room some twenty to twenty-six degrees colder than the womb.

Through the years, as the infants grow first into children and then into teen-agers, they encounter and adjust to a combination of circumstances and influences that *no other person on earth has ever experienced.* All of these individuals are unique, and day by day their personalities are being formed in complex ways.

The basic emotional-intellectual-physical self is quite well determined by the time children are six. By age fourteen their basic personality traits are solidified. They can change many of their ideas and attitudes as they develop and encounter new experiences, but the fundamental structure is now solidly in place.

And you had hoped, with a few well chosen words, to effect a radical change in someone's personality? You can abandon that notion. Changes do come about in human personalities, but when they do it is almost always because the person in question has *decided* to change.

We humans have a vested interest in remaining just as we are. The thought of a radical personality change is perceived as a threat by the average person. Pain—emotional, circumstantial, or physical—is the one great motivator. The dull throb of frustration, or the sharp stab of a crisis, can give us the impetus to change. But little else does.

GETTING PEOPLE TO CHANGE THEIR MINDS

Even though it is well-nigh impossible to effect a basic personality change in another person, it is sometimes possible to talk someone into a course of action that he or she had not expected to take.

A woman I knew wanted her husband to be more than a salesman, for she had expensive tastes and an eye for the social whirl. She persuaded him, over a period of several years, to go into business. He borrowed heavily on his life insurance and put a second mortgage on their home. They borrowed substantial amounts from her parents and his. Eventually they opened a new business. Eighteen months later they went into bankruptcy. It took them eleven years to recover financially. A very convincing woman became a sadder and wiser one.

I recall a father and mother who had high expectations for their rather passive son. They used the usual rewards for good grades, penalties for poor ones. The son was a fair student, but he was not particularly gifted. His father had hoped he would try out for football. He tried half-heartedly but quit at the end of the first year. After two years in college he dropped out of school and joined a religious cult, where he is now a passive, obedient disciple of a charismatic cult leader.

It is not difficult to dominate quiet, passive, or dependent people. A strong personality can easily take over a conversation. An average parent has little trouble overwhelming or coercing a child. But tragedy can result from forcing one's opinions or standards on others. How can one person ever be absolutely certain what is good for another? Many issues need to be resolved through relaxed communication.

Sometimes brainstorming can be more productive than confrontation: "Let's sit down and talk about it and see what the options are. You take one side, I'll take the other; then after a while we'll reverse sides and see if we can come up with some helpful ideas." This is a far better approach in many instances than the domineering, hard-nosed method.

MAKE AN ALLY OF YOUR ENEMY

During World War II, when gasoline was rationed and coupons were required, an acquaintance of mine desperately needed more gasoline for his business calls. He drove into a gasoline station and said, "Fill it up." When the attendant came to ask for the gas ration coupons, Harry was standing by the car.

"Got the stamps?" the attendant asked.

Pulling out a .32 automatic, Harry said, "Here's my coupon; now back away. I'm driving out of here."

Just as he turned to get into the car, the six-foot-four station owner came up behind him and hit him over the head with a heavy wrench. Harry collapsed, and they called an ambulance.

Later, Harry's wife asked me to visit him in the hospital. I found him lying in bed in a locked, barred room. Pale and meek, as well as weak, he looked up at me and said, "I guess I did something pretty dumb, huh?"

"How do you feel?" I asked.

"Rocky. That guy must have hit me pretty hard. What do you think they'll do to me?"

"For armed robbery? That's a felony. They send people to San Quentin for that."

"Yeah . . . What's going to happen to my wife and kids?"

I said I would see what I could do.

Harry was not the smartest man in town. In fact, he was a rather dull but basically well-intentioned person. Financial worries had simply unhinged him temporarily. I felt that it would be a terrible miscarriage of justice to send him to San Quentin. He needed psychiatric care more than a prison sentence.

A few days later I phoned the district attorney for an appointment. He wasn't exactly my enemy, but he was going to be on the other side of the fence, and I wanted him as an ally. I asked Harry's wife and two small children to come along with me on my little errand. On the day of the appointment the frail, frightened wife and the two scared little kids entered the D.A.'s office with me.

"Mr. Blanchard," I began, "we need your advice. You know about Harry, who held up a gas station attendant recently. He's in the hospital with a cracked skull. I know it is your duty to prosecute him, for he has done an illegal thing. However, I also know your reputation as a just and kind district attorney. So I want your advice regarding an attorney to defend Harry. You are obligated to prosecute him, but I know you want the best for everyone concerned.

"If Harry goes to San Quentin, his business will close and his family will have to go on welfare. My feeling is that Harry needs psychiatric care more than a jail sentence. Will you give me the names of two or three lawyers you would care to recommend?"

GETTING PEOPLE TO WORRY WITH YOU

The D.A. looked at the ceiling for a moment. "Well, there's Frank Jones . . . but no, he and the judge don't get along too well. Let's try Larry Ballentine. Yes, I think he'd do a good job."

The two children huddled around the mother, not understanding what was going on but sensing that it was something pretty bad. I was sorry to involve them, but I wanted the D.A. to see them.

The case never came to trial. The D.A. asked that a court-appointed psychiatrist interview Harry in the hospital. There was a recommendation for probation, and Harry was back home by the time his injury had healed.

This episode was, in a sense, a confrontation. There was no manipulation, no argument. But with a bit of logic and an appeal to the D.A.'s better nature, Harry was quite rightly spared a jail sentence. He was never in trouble again.

I can think of scores of times when I have said or done the wrong thing in a confrontation, and of other times when my performance was something less than ideal. But I have always felt satisfied with my appeal to the D.A.

The human personality consists of roughly four-fifths emotions and one-fifth intellect. This means that our decisions are arrived at on the basis of 80 percent emotion and only 20 percent intellect. To engage in a confrontation, or even a discussion, without taking emotions into account is to be only 20 percent effective in your dealings with people. By appealing to the D.A.'s emotional nature as well as to his basic sense of fair play, justice was done.

GETTING ALONG WITH THE OPPOSITION

Franklin Delano Roosevelt once related how he dealt with a troublesome senator. At a time when this balky senator was standing in the way of some vital legislation, he discovered that the man was an avid stamp collector, and he used that knowledge to great advantage.

One night when Roosevelt was working on his own stamp collection, he phoned the senator and asked for his help. Flattered, the senator came over that evening, and they worked together for a while. The next day, when a roll call vote was taken on the bill, the senator voted for it.

The lesson here is an important one. At no time during that philatelic session had either man mentioned their differences over the bill. They had simply gotten to know each other better, and the "enemy" had become a "friend."

SOME PRACTICAL DON'TS

Here are some "don'ts" that are helpful to remember when dealing with an opponent, whether the person is an enemy or merely someone you want to persuade.

1. *Don't expect logic or argument to eradicate a deep-seated neurosis.*

The compulsive liar, eater, talker, or drinker can never be dissuaded from a course of action by nagging or logic. Such approaches as these are futile:

"Don't you realize you're ruining your health?"

"Can't you see that you dominated the conversation with your incessant talking?"

"All you have to do to lose weight is to stop eating so much."

"Don't worry so much. Just learn to relax."

2. *Don't try too hard to win attention, laughter, or applause.*

You will win more friends if you will learn to be a good listener and let others shine, too.

3. *Don't wait for others to greet you.*

You can learn to be more outgoing by reaching out, taking the first step, being the first to greet others. One of my counselees said, "When I enter a room full of people, if no one rushes over to greet me, I get angry. I know it is ridiculous, but I can't help it."

"Do you ever greet people first?"

"No. I'm too timid."

"Do you feel others have the responsibility to reach out to you first?"

"Yes, isn't that stupid? But that is the way I feel."

This woman had to learn to force herself to reach out, to greet others first.

4. *Don't join the "vicious circle" of gossip mongers and character assassins.*

Dull people talk about people, intelligent people discuss ideas, and growing people talk about feelings.

5. *Don't try to get people to undertake more than they can comfortably accomplish.*

They may succeed, but they will be uncomfortable— and they may possibly hate you for it.

6. *Don't dominate the conversation.*

Give others a chance and you will be liked for the person you are, rather than resented for the way you took over the conversation.

7. *Don't become a negative, critical person.*

People are attracted to a positive personality, repelled by a negative one.

8. *Don't be afraid to admit it when you are wrong.*

Nothing is more ridiculous than a person who is obviously in the wrong insisting vehemently that he or she is right. This is a sure way to lose influence and credibility.

9. *Don't be afraid to be gentle.*

The strong can afford gentleness.

10. *Don't underestimate the importance of being a good listener.*

A TAPE-RECORDED MONOLOGUE

A young woman in great distress over her marriage made an appointment to see me. She sat down, plugged in her tape recorder, and announced that she didn't want to miss a single word that I had to say. I asked her to tell me about her problem. She began talking and continued without interruption for nearly fifty minutes.

As the hour was drawing to a close, I asked, "What are your options?" She named three.

"Which one seems to be the most reasonable course of action?" I asked.

"The third," she said without hesitation. She smiled, and took a deep breath. "I think I've found my answer." Then she turned off the tape recorder, told me how much she appreciated my help, and left.

This is not unusual. Often I ask probing questions, and sometimes I offer alternate suggestions as possibilities. In the above case, the young woman had a need to clarify her own thinking by having an interested listener.

Her mother had given her hours of advice and warnings. Her husband had made tearful pleas and promises. Another man with whom she thought she was in love had offered many inducements. But no one else had listened. In the end, she found that she had the answer—deep within herself.

Learning to be a good listener is just as important as knowing when and how to confront someone. There is a time and place for both in the incredibly complex realm of human relationships.

Psychologist Manuel J. Smith points out that everyone has certain important rights. He calls them "A Bill of Assertive Rights":

I. You have the right to judge your own behavior, thoughts, and emotions, and to take the responsibility for their initiation and consequences upon yourself.

II. You have the right to offer no reasons or excuses for justifying your behavior.

III. You have the right to judge whether you are responsible for finding solutions to other people's problems.

IV. You have the right to change your mind.

V. You have the right to make mistakes—and be responsible for them.

VI. You have the right to say, "I don't know."

VII. You have the right to be independent of the goodwill of others before coping with them.

VIII. You have the right to be illogical in making decisions.

IX. You have the right to say, "I don't understand."

X. You have the right to say, "I don't care."

You have the right to say no, without feeling guilty. [1]

> The greatest discovery of our generation is
> that human beings, by changing the inner
> attitudes of their minds, can change the outer
> aspects of their lives.   —*William James*

---

9 • How Inferiority Feelings and Fear Hamper Relationships

On a fall trip through New England, the tour guide told us a true story about an elderly woman on a previous tour. One morning the woman complained of not having slept well. She was asked if the bed had been uncomfortable.

"Well, that wasn't the real problem," she replied. "When I went to my room last evening, I found there was no furniture in it—not even a bed. So I slept on the floor, and my back is killing me."

The tour guide was astounded. "Why didn't you tell me or complain to the desk clerk?" he asked.

"Well, you see," explained the woman, "I've never been a complainer, and I just didn't want to upset anybody."

That sounds incredible, but it is an excellent illustration of the lengths to which some people will go to avoid provoking a confrontation or making a scene.

Numerous books on assertiveness have been written, and a variety of assertiveness courses offered, in recent years. Many people could benefit from such a course.

Some years ago on the "Candid Camera" TV program, a long line of people was shown waiting patiently at the supermarket checkout counter. Suddenly a brash young man carrying a bag of groceries abruptly pushed ahead of everyone until he stood at the head of the line. Several people glared at him, but all accepted his conduct without protest. No one challenged him. They put up with his rude behavior without verbal complaint. A few muttered under their breath, *but no one did anything*.

It was a setup, of course, staged to depict the way people behave under such circumstances.

Why are so many humans afraid to assert themselves? We seem to be divided into four general classifications.

There are those who, like the elderly woman who slept on the floor, patiently endure almost anything without complaint.

Another category consists of those who grumble a bit later, but who make no verbal protest at the time when they are being dealt with rudely or unjustly.

A third group is comprised of a minority who overreact strongly in such a situation and engage in verbal or physical conflict.

A still smaller segment of the population, under conditions such as those depicted on "Candid Camera," will quietly but firmly insist that the offending boor go back to the end of the line.

Both the way we were dealt with as children and the example our parents set have a great deal to do with the way we react in such situations.

My basic tendency, like that of a majority of people, is to put up with a certain amount of discomfort, rude behavior, or mistreatment—fuming inside—before asserting myself. When I finally do lodge a complaint, it may occasionally tend to be an overreaction.

The Right to Complain

One fall my wife Isobel and I were in a large New York City hotel. At dusk the room grew cold, and I tried fruitlessly to find a way to turn on some heat. Thinking that the heat would ultimately come on, we waited. Nothing happened.

Finally I called the desk and was told to call the engineer. I did so and was told that he couldn't turn on the heat until the temperature had dropped to a certain point. I said, "My friend, I do not intend paying for the privilege of freezing tonight. I want some heat." He replied that he was not authorized to turn it on.

I hung up and fumed for a time, getting colder all the while. Finally I called the engineer again and asked who could authorize him to get some heat up. He said the assistant manager could do so.

I got the assistant manager on the phone. His telephone manner was akin to that of the typical hotel desk clerk: aloof, cool, mildly insolent, and quite indifferent. (There must be a school where such people are trained in impersonal aloofness. I often get the feeling when checking in or out of even the finest hotels that personnel at the various desks are grossly irritated at being interrupted and bored with their jobs, and fervently wish I would go away.)

I told the assistant manager that we were cold, and asked if he would please authorize the engineer to turn on some heat. Brusquely and defensively, he stated that he had just told the engineer to do so. Translation: "Now that there is a complaint, I will do something about it." There was soon heat in our room.

Later a hotel maid came to the door to bring towels, and said, "Oh, you've got heat in here. Everyone has been complaining." They had complained to her, but none had lodged a complaint where it mattered—with the management. Why are most humans so nonassertive?

AFRAID OF NOT BEING "NICE"

Some people equate nonassertiveness with being long-suffering and make a Christian virtue out of it.

The apostle Paul urged the Christians at Ephesus to be "longsuffering,"[1] but a better translation of the word is *patience*. He tells us that, in an encounter with Peter, "I opposed him in public, because he was clearly wrong."[2] He could be assertive when it was appropriate, yet incredibly patient.

Letting yourself be run over, abused, and generally mistreated is no virtue. It is a serious personality defect. Enduring unavoidable hardship without complaint is certainly commendable, but putting up meekly with injustice is weakness.

Our rationalizations are numerous:

"I don't want to make a fuss; things will get better."

"I'll just put up with it; things aren't all that bad."

"I don't want to start an argument."

But those are not the real reasons.

Basically, we are so afraid of not being "nice"— meaning nonassertive—and so desperately need to be liked and loved, that we put up with inconsiderateness and mistreatment rather than protest.

On a cruise ship the steward gave our party a slip suggesting the amount of the tip we were to give. Apparently some in the group did not give a large enough tip to satisfy him, so he refused to return our passports until we complied. Several of us made up the required amount and smoothed the affair over.

After returning home I brooded over this mistreatment. Finally I informed the travel agent, who lodged a complaint with the steamship company. We were told later that the steward had been fired. My mistake was in not complaining immediately to the ship's captain, but perhaps delayed action is better than none at all.

A friend of mine—a loving, gentle, but very frank and open person—was present at an all-day denominational meeting at which I was presiding. An official from national headquarters had been droning on endlessly for an hour and a half. The audience was bored and restless. I could see that the official was trying to kill a controversial measure by talking it to death.

Finally, without waiting for the speaker to reach a period or even a comma, my friend arose and said quite loudly, "This is killing me, and I am going home." Then

137

he stalked out. The speaker very quickly wound down his interminable discourse.

Later I congratulated my friend on his courage and succinctness. I have never forgotten the relief that showed on the faces of the bored-to-death conference people when he expressed their sentiments so beautifully. My friend was the only one who had the courage to object to an oratorical absurdity.

At the root of this and all such related problems is the fact that most people feel some degree of inferiority or inadequacy, which manifests itself as timidity. Few people enjoy making a scene or engaging in a noisy argument. But there are quiet ways of standing up firmly for oneself and one's rights. No one has to put up with insolence, inefficiency, or stupidity.

How Much Shall We Put Up With?

At a brunch buffet counter I observed that there were no eggs left on the tray. I pointed this out to the young woman in charge. She said insolently, "There's plenty there."

I said, "Fragments, scraps. I'd like some eggs." She shrugged and started to walk away.

I took her arm and asked quietly, "What is your name?"

Her eyes widened, and she said, "Carol." I took out my pen and wrote it down. She rushed off to the kitchen and returned immediately with a large tray of scrambled eggs.

I dislike doing things like that. I prefer peace and harmony, and I don't enjoy making anyone unhappy. This springs from my early childhood, when I learned not to complain or talk back or ask for things. That insidious tape is still playing, and I mute it only by an act of will.

"Ask ... Seek ... Knock ..."

Jesus said, "Ask, and you will receive; seek, and you will find; knock, and the door will be opened to you."[3] This is usually interpreted as meaning that we are to *ask God*. But it is not so stated. My interpretation might be

138

open to question, but I think it quite possible that Jesus was stating an all-encompassing principle that can apply just as well to human relations as to relationships between humans and God.

Let us suppose for a moment that Jesus is suggesting, in part, that one must be prepared to *ask for one's rights,* to seek until one finds a way, to knock on doors until persistence finally pays off. Quiet persistence can be a very great virtue when it is appropriate.

ASKING FAVORS

One aid in making friends is to ask people *to do you a favor.* Obviously this must be done with care. I am not suggesting that we become manipulative, using people for our own purposes.

I recall a man in my church who seemed quite aloof. It wasn't clear to me whether he disliked me or was simply diffident. Learning that he loved gardening, I asked him one day if he would take a look at my lawn some Saturday afternoon and give me some advice on what to do about some large brown spots. He agreed quite readily. He came, and when he got to talking about lawns—a subject on which he was quite knowledgeable—he came alive. We became friends. As with many people, his seeming aloofness, often mistaken for hauteur, simply masked his lack of self-confidence.

Such people are usually lonely and long for acceptance. They would give almost anything to have a spontaneous, outgoing personality.

No one is ever insulted by having his or her opinion asked. Most people are pleased to be able to help you. It places them in the superior position of *giver*, while you are in the position of *receiver*.

Unfortunately, many people with a deep-seated inferiority complex seem unable to ask for help, or to ask for anything, for that matter. They feel unworthy. "Oh, they wouldn't want to do anything for *me,*" is their feeling.

The exception to this rule is the human leech, who cannot accept love but can ask and ask and ask, endlessly, piteously. Gifts and favors are the only form of love that such persons can receive.

In human relationships there is a time to "give and it will be given unto you," and a time to "ask and it shall be given." These are universal truths to help us in our relationships with other people.

WHEN FRIENDLY GESTURES ARE REJECTED

Our plane had stopped at Athens for refueling on the way to Jerusalem. As I got up to go for a brief walk, I glanced behind me at a couple who looked like Americans. I said as I arose, "I see you people are Americans."

The man looked stonily ahead; the woman said in crisp British tones, looking over my head, "We're not." They both turned and looked out the window.

My seatmate happened to be a very outgoing English salesman. I asked him, "What is it that makes it so difficult to open a conversation with some English people?"

He said, "Oh, that's easy. Lots of our people are afraid. They don't know how to open a conversation. They aren't stuck up; they're just inhibited, and they'd give anything to be as open as I am, for instance. I've had to learn to be more spontaneous in my line of work, but some of us never learn the art."

Later I turned and said to the couple, half facetiously, "I apologize for thinking that you were Americans."

The woman replied icily, "It's not necess'ry."

My English friend said, "It's no use. Some people just don't know how to relate easily. Sad."

Fear and inferiority feelings are inextricably linked. Fear of failure, of appearing ridiculous, of criticism, of rejection, are all tied in with an underlying sense of inferiority.

THE MOST COMMON FEARS

There are other fears that limit our effectiveness. Some researchers questioned three thousand people about their worst fears. Many named more than one fear. These were the results of the survey:

Biggest Fear	Percent Naming It
1. Speaking before a group	41
2. Heights	32
3. Insects and bugs	22
4. Financial problems	22
5. Deep water	22
6. Sickness	19
7. Death	19
8. Flying	18
9. Loneliness	14
10. Dogs	11
11. Driving/riding in a car	9
12. Darkness	8
13. Elevators	8
14. Escalators	5

If you have some particular fear listed here, join the club. Our membership is vast.

Fear of speaking before a group stems from fear of ridicule, of failure, of being the focus of attention. It can also result from self-consciousness.

Fear of heights has any of a number of sources: fear of "falling morally"; an actual deficiency in one's sense of balance; childhood panic carried over into adult life, and many others.

Extreme fear of water can originate in a near-drowning episode; in a deep fear of emotions (water symbolizes emotions), or from being encouraged to swim at too young an age.

Fear of elevators or other small enclosed spaces (claustrophobia) often originates in a specific episode (such as being locked in a closet). Sometimes it can be displaced from some long forgotten experience in childhood.

There is a reason for everything, and one need not feel ashamed of some apparently irrational fear.

Because there is a universal need to be significant, important, loved, admired, accepted, approved, it follows that there is an enormous amount of felt inferiority floating around. A given person may not *be* inferior in any sense; friends and associates may vote him or her to be the most admired and most successful person in his or her area. But psychological tests reveal that often very gifted people have inferiority feelings. One may be greatly admired, yet feel inadequate and fearful in certain situations.

FICKLE FAME

Fame, which is so ardently pursued by some, can be a very fragile, fickle thing. Raquel Welch, sex symbol of the late sixties, complained that "sex symbols are vulnerable and tragic figures who have a corner on the misery market." A widely acclaimed TV actress declares that "when you are a celebrity, you are totally a victim."

Nevertheless, as Susan Margolis once observed, "the gifted as well as the deranged around us are struggling to be famous the way earlier Americans struggled to be saved."

Some cynic has remarked that in a future society, everyone will be famous for fifteen minutes.

GOSSIP AND INFERIORITY

I was tremendously impressed years ago by the reaction of a great man to insidious gossip. A Louisville, Kentucky, paper had printed some scurrilous gossip about Dr. E. Y. Mullins, then president of the Southern Baptist Theological Seminary. In chapel one morning he opened the session for questions.

One student asked, "Dr. Mullins, how do you feel about the terrible things the press is saying about you?"

His reply was a classic: "Those people have dipped into the garbage pail of their imagination and drawn up morsels to their own taste. Next question." The student body was stunned for a moment by the brevity and force of his response, then broke into spontaneous applause.

A dramatic and rather frightening illustration of the power of gossip was reported in *Time* magazine:

> Somebody told somebody that Mabel Sheehan, 72, who lives alone with her sheep dog in a working-class district of Philadelphia, had bought a car for a friend. Somebody else heard that she had paid for several trips to Puerto Rico for other friends. None of this was true, police said later.
>
> But people in the neighborhood began estimating how much money she might have stashed away in her modest house. Someone guessed $35,000. Someone guessed more. There was even talk of a hoard of $45 million. None of this was true, either—her only income is her monthly $247 Social Security check, and her only savings consists of a pre-paid burial—but when the rumors started spreading . . . a crowd of 300 curiosity-seekers gathered in front of the house.
>
> It required 100 police, on horses and in riot gear, to protect the house from vandalism. One spectator asked, "If there's no money in there, why are all these police guarding the house?"
>
> Mrs. Sheehan fled to a convent for safety, 19 persons were arrested, and police spent the entire day persuading the crowd that the rumors were all false. [4]

So much for human nature and gossip.

There appears to be no limit to the human tendency to gossip, speculate, and meddle in the lives of others. Someone wrote to "Dear Abby" and stated that some neighbors had bought an expensive home, paying cash. They seemed weird. They didn't have a TV, according to their little boy, and had only one car in their two-car garage. Children and mother used the bus and rarely went anywhere except to church. The wife wore no jewelry and had no fancy clothes, and the children were permitted to have no toys dealing with war or violence. "Could they belong to some offbeat religious cult?" the questioner asked.

The columnist replied: "Maybe they've just got cash, conservative standards, high moral principles and pacifist ideals. They sound like ideal neighbors to me."

Greed, avarice, jealousy, possessiveness, insecurity, suspicion—all these emotions lie tangled at the roots of human inferiority feelings. The sad thing is that in some degree, large or small, all of us are infected with the disease. To feel inferior is part of the human condition.

If you want to help people who suffer from inferiority feelings and all of the problems resulting from that difficulty, there are certain pitfalls to avoid.

First, *do not make an effort to change them.* You cannot change other people, whether by direct action or by subterfuge. Trying to do so will only make them angry. However, others may change in response to an open and loving attitude on your part.

Second, *help people on your own terms, not theirs.* Only you know how much time, energy, money, love, or sympathy you have available. Some people who ask for a loan need to learn how to handle a budget and live within their income. Some who ask for sympathy or love or attention may be bottomless pits that can never be filled. Such people need intensive therapy.

Third, *advice may or may not be indicated.* Some ask for it and "but" you to death, responding to each proffered bit of advice with, "Yes, but. . . ."

The callous or indifferent give the brush-off to people asking for help. The compassionate often get caught up in a fruitless and endless effort to help them. One woman reported that she had listened for one to three hours every day for two years as a neighbor poured out her marital difficulties. The problem was never resolved, of course. One must determine how best to spend one's resources of time and energy and compassion, and not get trapped by a masochistic "sapper."

A masochist is a person who unconsciously derives pleasure from pain. A psychic masochist may be accident prone, trouble prone, disease prone, failure prone, or bad judgment prone. People of this type long for happiness and fulfillment. However, they do not feel they deserve it, and they actually attract trouble. Helped from one disaster, they soon find themselves involved in another.

The causes are complex, but one frequent source is a deep feeling of inferiority that seems to invite problems.

When you encounter such a person, do not waste your energies trying to solve his or her problem. Such individuals desperately need intensive therapy.

DIFFERENT KINDS OF PRIDE

False pride, an effort to compensate for deep feelings of inferiority, often originates in a warped childhood. But there is another kind of pride that needs to be considered. Hans Selye comments on this:

> Pride in excellence . . . is a primeval biological feeling; it is not limited to our species. Even a hunting dog is proud to bring in his quarry unscathed; just look at his face and you will see that his work has made him happy. A performing seal is manifestly pleased by earning applause. Only the stress of frustration, of lack of purpose, can spoil the satisfaction of performance. . . . Man must have recognition; he cannot tolerate constant censure, for that is what—more than any other stressor—makes work frustrating and harmful for him.[5]

Pride in a job well done, in a significant achievement, in attaining some long-sought goal, is a worthy emotion. Call it satisfaction, a feeling of well-being, pleasure, or feeling good about some achievement, it amounts to the same thing. But, of course, any virtue pushed to the extreme or the ridiculous becomes a vice.

Being inordinately proud may arouse either the envy or the hatred of others. One man who seemed to consistently attract good fortune said, "When someone congratulates me on my good luck, I usually respond with, 'Yes, but I have to have this big root canal job, and business isn't too good just now.' It makes them feel better to know that I've got problems. I don't want people to envy me. There is a certain amount of hostility in envy, and I don't want that."

SUCCESS WITHOUT A FORMAL EDUCATION

I have often heard people lament the fact that they didn't have a college education, the inference being that, if they had gone to college, things would have been vastly different. That isn't necessarily so. I remind such people that Eleanor Roosevelt never attended college. Nor did Grover Cleveland, Joseph Conrad, or Amelia Earhart. Kahlil Gibran never got a college education, nor did Ernest Hemingway, Rudyard Kipling, H. L. Mencken, John D. Rockefeller, George Bernard Shaw, Dylan Thomas, or Harry S. Truman. None of them was ever heard to express regret about this.

High school dropouts have included such prominent people as Henry Ford, George Gershwin, Jack London, Rod McKuen, Steve McQueen, Will Rogers, William Saroyan, Frank Sinatra, and Wilbur and Orville Wright. Ray Kroc, founder and chairman of the board of McDonald's, was also a high school dropout.

This need not serve as encouragement to drop out of school; the more education one acquires, the better. Yet the lack of an education need not be a deterrent.

THE BIG HANDICAP

Our feelings of inferiority or inadequacy, fear of failure or rejection, constitute a greater handicap than lack of an education. Today in our society, just about anyone who wants an education can get one; but not everyone finds it as easy to overcome a debilitating sense of inferiority.

There are people who are so constituted by a fortunate combination of heredity, environment, and determination that they will succeed with or without a formal education.

The kind of determination and native ability exhibited by Admiral Hyman Rickover would enable almost anyone to succeed. Admiral Rickover is the father of the nuclear submarine, without which we would be a very vulnerable nation. Over the strong opposition of Congress and the Navy brass, he fought single-handedly for construction of the first nuclear-powered submarine. At times he stood absolutely alone. He was, and at times still is, a very unpopular man. Yet he is still needling where it is required—prodding, pushing, exhorting.

To explain why he continues after thirty years to battle for his vision of a Navy whose major fighting ships are nuclear powered, Admiral Rickover tells an odd and touching story, a parable about an ancient philosopher who came to a city to save its people from their sins. At first the inhabitants of the city listened to him. But gradually they turned away. One day a child asked the learned man why he went on—did he not see that his mission was hopeless? As Rickover tells it, the philosopher replied, "In the beginning, I thought I could change men. If I still shout, it is only to prevent men from changing me."

ONLY HUMANS BUILD COMPUTERS

The Cyber 76 computer can perform twelve million operations *per second*. It costs thirteen million dollars. We stand in awe of such performance. After all, no human mind can begin to match the feats of that computer. But, lest we abase ourselves too much before a piece of metal, remember this: *Only a human mind could conceive and build such a machine.* No matter how limited a person may be in intellect, education, or opportunity, his or her mind can do many things that a thirteen-million-dollar computer cannot do.

Besides, it is made in the image of a clumsy, earlier generation computer, and we are made in the image of God, a little lower than the angels. We are immortal, and we will be living and growing and singing God's praises when earth's finest computer is rusting away in the ruins of a city whose name will have long since been forgotten.

Rejoice in that, my friend. "To whom much is given, of him will much be required."[6] The corollary of that is that if you were less endowed, less will be required of you. Use what you have and do not grovel before the better educated, the great achievers, the famous. In heaven we shall all be stripped of our achievements and judged on the basis of what we are and how well we have lived up to our potential, considering our limitations and handicaps.

Rejoice! You are an all-right person. You can be inferior only in your own sight.

> A philosopher is a person who gives other
> people advice about troubles he hasn't had.
> —*William R. Lewis*

10 • Reactions and Responses

My wife, Isobel, and I were traveling on one of those marvelously fast and efficient Japanese trains from Tokyo to Nikko to see a famous shrine.

After we were well under way, a very pleasant stewardess served tea, which I thought a delightful custom. I enjoyed the small cup of tea so much that I motioned to the young stewardess and asked if I might have a second cup. Her initial look of surprise changed quickly to one of utter confusion. I perceived immediately that I had broken some nine-thousand-year-old social custom. Not knowing just how, I waited to see what was going to happen.

A sudden conference was called at the end of the car. Two stewards and our stewardess conversed in excited tones. I sensed that whatever social blunder I had inadvertently committed must have been a big one.

After a long discussion one of the stewards approached me and said, with some embarrassment, "I am so very sorry, but if you want another cup, it will be necessary for you to *pay* for it." He seemed to be terribly grieved to have to impart this information to me, for he was wringing his hands nervously. Apparently this was the first time the grave issue had arisen in his lifetime, and he wasn't precisely sure how it should be handled.

I smiled and said, "No problem," and handed him a dollar bill. He looked confused, and then I realized that they were not accustomed to making change, since one cup of tea was complimentary and no charge had ever been made. But after another hurried top-level conference at the end of the car, a price was decided upon, and he brought me a handful of yen while the young stewardess poured us some more tea.

NEW SITUATIONS

How do you handle an unfamiliar situation?

A few fortunate people are so secure in themselves, and react with such spontaneity, that they confront any new problem or situation with calm assurance. The rest of us have, let us say, 120 possible situations catalogued. We know from experience how we will handle them, because we have been confronted by each one often enough that it poses no problem to us. But when Number 121 arises, we may react with anything from surprise to panic.

When our thought patterns or habits are suddenly challenged by something strange, a monkey wrench is thrown into the mental machinery and confusion results. Our reactions may vary, depending on the circumstances.

I was buying a new car, and for once in my life intended to pay cash for it. The only problem was that the car was ready for delivery sooner than expected, and the cash I needed wouldn't be available for ninety days. Banks have few ways of making money except by lending it, so I went to a branch of the bank I had done business with for more than forty years and explained my problem. There had been a big turnover of bank officials, so I found myself dealing with a new man. He looked at me with calm, cool indifference.

I thought of the story of the man who was applying for a bank loan. The banker had a glass eye, of which he was inordinately proud. It looked quite natural, but apparently he had some need for reassurance. He said to the applicant, "I'll tell you what I'll do. I have one glass eye. If you can tell me which one it is, I'll lend you the money."

Without hesitation the man said, "It's your left one."

"Right! How can you tell?"

"Easy," he said. "It's the friendlier-looking one."

The man I was dealing with didn't have a glass eye, but he showed neither warmth nor friendliness. When I explained the situation, he said, "On a loan of that nature you'd have to bring us a financial statement."

"Look," I said, "this is a simple auto loan, for ninety days. It would take me at least two hours to fill out the kind of financial statement you want, and I am short of time." I was getting irritated.

"Sorry," he said, "we have our rules."

"My friend," I responded, "I've been doing business with this bank for more than forty years. I've lived two blocks from here for thirty years and am gainfully employed. I wouldn't consider making out a financial statement for a simple loan like this." And I stalked out, quietly seething.

As I got into my car, I thought, "Now, that was an immature way to react. It was absurd to become so indignant. The banker's reaction was just as absurd. But if I were to meet that man at a social function or at church, I'd feel pretty stupid.

Then I realized what had happened. First, I had a back problem, and I was in considerable pain. I was also in a hurry, for I was late for another appointment. Most important of all, I was baffled by a situation with which I had never before been confronted. Because of all these things my response to it was quite inappropriate.

In situations of this nature, it is seldom a matter of who is right and who is wrong. The question is, was the response appropriate?

HUSBAND-AND-WIFE REACTIONS WITH GOLF CLUBS

Sometimes it isn't a strange situation that baffles us, but a familiar one we've never resolved.

The situation: John, with golf clubs in hand, opens the door, ready to leave for his regular Saturday morning golf game. Mary says, with some asperity, "John, you didn't take out the garbage like you said you would. I asked you twice last night, remember?"

The problem: Mary has to stay home with three children while John is out enjoying himself with his friends on the golf links. Verbally she encourages him to play golf, as he needs the recreation. But unconsciously she resents staying home while he's out having fun. The garbage is a pretext. Daily she handles huge bags of groceries weighing four times as much as the garbage can, and John knows this.

John, frozen at the door with quiet indignation, is aware that the garbage is only an oblique way of throwing obstacles in the way of his Saturday plans. He also recalls that he has promised for the past six weeks to fix one of the children's bikes, to repair the garage door, and to remedy a leaky faucet. He feels resentful and guilty and is therefore immobilized. Anger is the top emotion, the one of which he is most conscious. What are his options?

Option Number One: He can say, with ill-concealed hostility, "Take it out yourself. You're not crippled. You know good and well you're just doing this because you resent my playing golf on Saturday." Not good. It doesn't take into account his guilty feelings about the household jobs he has failed to take care of. Besides, she'll be cool and distant when he comes home tonight if he responds that way.

Option Number Two: He can take out the garbage, saying nothing but letting his face and body language convey the hostility he feels. This isn't a good option, either. It does nothing to solve the problem of her regularly throwing obstacles in the way of his golf game. And, it does nothing for his anger and his guilty feelings about the neglected household chores.

Option Number Three: Pause. "What am I feeling? I'm mad. The fellows are waiting for me; I'm already late. Why am I mad? Because Mary does this consistently, and because I've been avoiding those distasteful little picayune repair jobs I hate. I don't have time to thrash this out with her right now. I will take out the garbage and try to avoid showing the anger I don't have time to discuss. I'll talk it out with her tonight."

That night: "Did you have a nice golf game, dear?"

"Only fair. I sliced a lot, and my score was worse than usual. I think it was because I was still mad about the garbage."

"Garbage?" (Very innocently.)

"Yeah. I was really pushed out of shape this morning when you stopped me at the door with the old garbage can bit. I honestly felt that it was your standard way of expressing resentment about the fact that I can get away to play golf on Saturday while you stay home with the kids. But I also recognized that I felt guilty about taking the day off to play golf when I had failed to keep my promise about fixing some things around the house—like Jerry's bike, the leaky faucet, and the garage door. So I'm mad at myself, and at you. Mostly at myself, I think."

"But John, I had asked you to take out the garbage, and you'd promised, and . . ."

"Look, you're right, I just plain forgot. It's my fault. I hate that piddling chore as much as you do. It's my problem. However, I think we need to deal with your tendency to agree that I need a little recreation, then throw up road blocks as though you resented my golf. Let's talk about *your* recreational needs. If you don't get enough time off during the week when the kids are in school, I can spend part of the weekend with the kids and let you get some relief."

This can lead to a helpful discussion in which the basic issue can be resolved.

Here are the principles involved in working through such a conflict:

1. *Accept the fact that you're angry.* There is nothing inherently evil about *feeling* anger. It is when we express it destructively that it is wrong.

2. *Pause; wait.* Give yourself time to cool off and think it over before responding.

3. *Accept your own responsibility*. If you were partly to blame, admit it.

RESPONDING TO HURT AND REJECTION

A woman counselee, in discussing her childhood, told me how her family was excommunicated over a religious issue. When she was a little girl, a theological controversy had arisen between the church officials and her father. He had stated in a sermon that the act of redemption was complete when Jesus, on the cross, uttered the words, "It is finished." Later he was confronted by officials of his denomination, who believed that redemption was not final until the spear actually pierced Jesus' side, and He died. There had been a furious altercation.

I felt comfortable enough about my relationship with this woman to laugh. Then she laughed, and we both laughed together hilariously, over the ancient theological ruckus. Finally I asked her, "How did you feel when your family was excommunicated?"

"Terrible!" she replied. "I felt rejected, condemned, and very, very lonely. Most of all I felt badly for Daddy. He was crushed."

"That was many years ago. What do you feel now?"

She smiled. "Of course it's all right now. I feel nothing but pity for those pious legalists. I can laugh about it now. Time is really a great healer, isn't it?"

So, the initial response had been one of hurt and rejection. Then the healing force of time had made it all right. Or had it?

In one of her Primal Integration sessions later that week, the woman went back to age twelve and relived the event. At first there was hurt, and tears. She was feeling some of the rejection that she had not allowed herself to experience at the time. Then came anger—good, full-bodied, wholesome, healing rage. In daily life she was self-contained and quite reserved, but in her primal session she let loose all of the pent-up anger that had been repressed for more than forty years.

"That felt great!" she said when the session was over. "I had no idea I had buried all that anger. Just imagine

153

what it's been doing to me emotionally and spiritually all these years." She had traveled more than ten thousand miles expressly to get relief from her vague emotional distress. The hurt and anger she released in that one session was part of her healing.

Time does heal, at a conscious level. But it does not necessarily eradicate the original hurt. This woman had been urged by her father to forgive and forget, and she had done so to the best of her conscious ability. But her emotional structure still retained, at an unconscious level, some of the pain she had been unable to let herself feel at the time.

Why bother to dredge up forty-year-old hurts? The answer, of course, is that they are not dead hurts. The unresolved pain of the past is still there *unless dealt with fully at the time*. Further, it takes considerable psychic energy to hold down repressed emotions. This places a strain on the personality that can result in emotional or physical symptoms. When the psalmist prays, "Cleanse me of secret sins,"[1] he is asking to be cleansed of buried hurts and failures that he is unable to dredge up. God forgives our sins, whether remembered or forgotten; but we do not forgive ourselves for buried mistakes. They have to be dealt with for the sake of our own mental and emotional and spiritual health.

TAKING ORDERS

How well do you take orders? Everyone has to learn to obey orders. As children we are required to obey our parents and teachers. When employed, we take orders from the boss, who may not always be considerate of our feelings. We take orders from the government—local, state and federal. Even the stop and go signals give their quiet orders, and we instinctively obey them. The red curb issues a silent order, and we obey.

It would be a chaotic world if there were no orders: anarchy would result. Consequently most of us choose to obey the laws of society and any instructions issued by the person or firm employing us. However, not everyone enjoys taking orders.

I recall a cheerful young woman who was once employed briefly in our office. (I do not hire or fire the office employees. It is done by my associate director, who does it well.) At one point during the trial period, Mrs. Baker gave some instructions that the young woman didn't carry out. When Mrs. Baker patiently pointed out the mistake, the young woman said, rather flippantly, "Well, that's just a matter of opinion."

After that mistake and three or four others, she was let go. She had not learned the one basic rule for all employees: You have to follow instructions. You don't have to agree with them. You are free to think them a stupid idea or to offer alternate suggestions. But you are not free to disregard them.

Getting Fired Is No Fun

When I was working my way through college, I was employed for a time at a large department store in Chicago's Loop. I worked there mornings, from eight-thirty to twelve-thirty, and attended school afternoons. We spent the first half hour on the job arranging stock and began waiting on customers at nine o'clock.

I soon observed that it didn't take all four of us in the department to arrange the stock. This could easily be done by one or two persons. Because I had to get up rather early for a long ride on the elevated, I got into the habit of getting my breakfast at the store. I would punch in at 8:30, do a little work on the stock, then go upstairs to the Men's Grill for a quick breakfast. After all, there was nothing to do; the stock was all in good shape. I wasn't cheating anyone—or so I reasoned. But I was having breakfast on company time.

After Christmas, when the time came to let some clerks go, you can guess who was among the ones let out. Right. I was. My sales record was good, but my performance lacked integrity. I was using company time for my own purposes. Cheating is the proper word for it. I wasn't obeying company orders. I was fired—and quite rightly deserved it.

Some people are so constituted that they bitterly resent all authority. They may learn that, in order to survive, they must take orders from the boss, but inwardly they are resentful. That resentment can take several forms.

Some persons who quietly obey orders at work may come home and discharge the displaced anger on a husband or wife, or on the children.

Sometimes those who had rigid or authoritarian parents express their hostility to authority by rejecting God's authority. Quite unaware of the source of their resentment, they may become atheists and argue heatedly about the hypocrisy so evident among Christians. If more passive, they may simply refuse to have anything to do with religion.

As has been pointed out previously, all excessiveness originates in childhood. Therefore, when we discover in ourselves some aberrant behavior, some kind of excessiveness, it can be worthwhile to dig back into childhood to discover the source.

Unfortunately, the universal tendency to rationalize our behavior can prevent us from taking a clear, unbiased look at ourselves. Usually we need an objective, qualified person to assist us in this process.

THE PAST IS STILL IN US

Henry, a delightful young man in his early thirties, hated going to church with his wife but attended with her because she was so insistent. He always ended up Sunday afternoon with a splitting headache. In his primal sessions he discovered the reason for this.

When Henry was six, his father had died in an accident. His grandmother had assured him that, "God took your daddy; he's now with Jesus." This, to the six-year-old, made God a murderer. Henry needed a daddy; he didn't want him to be with Jesus. He hadn't wept at the funeral. In one primal session he reexperienced the long-forgotten feeling, "If I break down, my sister and my mother will, too. I have to be strong for them. I must

156

be a little man, like Grandma said, and men don't cry."

Since reliving that childhood trauma, Henry no longer hates going to church, nor does he suffer from headaches.

No matter how carefully we rationalize them, our responses and reactions have roots that go back to childhood. Jeanne had been hospitalized twice briefly because of her emotional outbursts. Once she had attempted suicide and very nearly succeeded. On another occasion she had left work and driven blindly until her car was out of gas, then phoned a local minister, in panic, to come and get her. He referred her to us.

In her therapy Jeanne relived two totally repressed incidents of being sexually molested. Then, with paralyzing intensity, she heard the fights between her mother and father. Finally she mourned the loss of her daddy, whom she loved, feared, and hated. Jeanne is now well and functions normally.

WHEN IS DIVORCE JUSTIFIED?

A woman called me long distance and talked for over an hour. She had read one of my books and mistakenly assumed that her complex marital situation might be resolved in a phone conversation.

Her husband, who professed to be a Christian, frequently knocked her down when she dared to disagree with his doctrinal views. He taught a Bible class consisting mostly of young women and spent a great many evenings counseling these women in their homes, often until quite late at night. He had beaten his children mercilessly. She cited half a dozen instances of mixed cruelty, weird reactions, and emotional instability.

The children were grown and she had a job, but she was uncertain whether or not to seek a divorce. She asked my advice.

From a distance of a thousand miles, and having heard only her side of the story, I felt incapable of giving any specific advice. But I did state a conviction: "If you fear for your physical safety, you have every right to ask him to move out. If your emotional well-being is threatened, by all means separate."

"But I don't believe in divorce," she said.

"I don't believe in the desirability of sin, suffering, and sorrow," I said, "but they are realities. We have diseases and accidents, and mentally unbalanced husbands. If you think he is acting irrationally, it is important that you save yourself."

I then referred her to one of our trainees living much closer and urged her to get some professional counseling.

WHEN RATIONAL JUDGMENT IS DIFFICULT

Sometimes a person can become so beaten down as to be incapable of making a rational decision.

A young mother whose husband had died reported to me that her husband's parents had been verbally abusive to her children. The mother was planning to take the children to another state, where she had the promise of a job. Fearful of losing touch with her grandchildren, the grandmother had said to one of them, "If you move there, you'll be dead in six months." The little boy was terrified and asked, "Mommy, is that true? Will I die?"

There were many other instances of emotional instability on the part of both grandparents. The mother, accordingly, told them that they could not visit her children so long as they were verbally threatening or abusive.

I said, "Under the circumstances you have stated, you were quite within your rights."

She said, "Oh, thank you! Everyone I've talked to has insisted that I am morally bound to let the children visit their grandparents."

Advice from friends, relatives, and neighbors can confuse an otherwise intelligent person so that he or she loses the capacity for rational judgment.

DEALING WITH PREJUDICE

Clyde was a man who hated three things: Jews, blacks, and prejudiced people, in that order. He employed some thirty men in his business. One day he announced to me that blacks were hopelessly lazy, irresponsible, and dishonest. How does one react to a statement like that?

I asked Clyde for the basis of his comment. His experience with blacks, I found, was limited to his contact with three employees. On the basis of that, he had formed some generalizations about all blacks. I wanted to tell him that his experience with them was too limited to form a valid judgment. I felt an urge to ask him if he would come to such conclusions if he had had a bad experience with three Irishmen, three Lutherans, or three Eskimos.

I knew, however, that this approach would get us nowhere. I reminded myself that I was not responsible for changing his mind, and that he was entitled to his opinion even if it seemed somewhat distorted to me.

Finally I said, "I grew up on the Mexican border. All of the Mexicans I knew were 'wetbacks' who had waded across the Rio Grande—peons fleeing terrible poverty. I formed my opinion of Mexicans as a whole from my limited contact with these few dozen poverty-stricken Mexicans. But after several visits to Mexico, covering a dozen or more cities, I completely revised my opinion of Mexicans. I then became a bit ashamed of my earlier opinion, which had been based on incomplete evidence."

My friendship with Clyde remained intact, but I question whether it would have if I had attacked his views and accused him of blatant prejudice.

THE RETIRED HUSBAND SYNDROME

A woman writing to columnist Abigail Van Buren complained about her husband in this manner:

Dear Abby: My husband is 72 and retired, but he's making a career out of making my life miserable. He used to be quite the man about town. I spent many lonely evenings wondering where he was and when he'd come home.

Now I can't get him out of the house. I actually have to look for things for him to do.

I can hardly stand the sight of him! My stomach turns over when I hear his key in the door.

After he reads the morning paper he follows me around supervising the cooking and housekeeping.

If a lady friend of mine comes over for a cup of tea, he horns in and monopolizes the conversation.

Dear God, I am so sick of him, death would be a welcome release!

Aging in Indiana

My wife tells me that some of her women friends who have retired husbands make the same complaint. How can a harassed wife react to such a situation?

One husband who was not retired, but who had an office at home, consistently followed his wife around the house—even into the bathroom. When she demanded some privacy and locked the bathroom door, he would drag his chair to the bathroom door, and sit reading his paper, and, when she emerged, ask, "What took you so long?"

It is often helpful to understand the personality make-up of this type of man. He is a passive, or passive-aggressive, person. Although he may have shown aggressive traits in business, part of his personality has been rendered passive. Often this is the result of a distorted relationship with the mother, or having been overmothered, or of having lost the mother when quite young. Such a man may have had a passive, inadequate, or absentee father. So he tries unconsciously to make a mommy out of his wife and is dependent upon her for guidance and support. This he would deny with his dying breath.

There is both good news and bad news regarding such men. First, the bad news. They do not readily change. Logic, argument, and reasoning are usually futile. The wife of such a man, driven to near-distraction by a cloying, clinging, dependent husband, can grow so irritated that she becomes sharp and rejecting. This worsens the situation. The husband then feels rejected and may withdraw into hurt, sullen silence for a time, only to resume his wife-trailing when he has recovered.

However, there is some hope. While the chances of a permanent cure are remote, I have known several wives who resolved the problem to some degree by finding things to do away from home.

Two of them, when fed up with excessive togetherness, simply took off. One who had relatives in the East would visit them for one to three months at a time. Another found herself a part-time job. Another hurried through her household duties, then rushed off to her volunteer work at a local hospital. Still another joined a women's bridge club that played twice a week. She also did a great deal of reading at the public library.

Do these seem like escape measures? That is precisely what they are. When an intolerable situation cannot otherwise be ameliorated, one can often embrace such an alternative.

One creative possibility, of course, is to seek the cooperation of a friendly minister and share the problem with him. If he is innovative, he can often find, or even invent, a job for a retired man.

I remember a group of retired persons, including several men, who came to the church office every Thursday morning, sat in the nearby church library, and folded the Sunday bulletins and weekly newsletters. We could easily have invested in a folding machine, but that would have deprived those lovely people of their weekly contribution and talkfest.

The human mind longs for happy endings. We automatically look for an amicable solution to any problem. The sad fact is that sometimes there is no such solution. Often in human relationships we have to adopt a realistic attitude such as the one our government has regarding Cuba and the Middle East.

Because Cuba is a suitable nearby base for Russian missiles and submarines, it is a threat to our national safety. At present there seems to be no viable solution to the problem.

In the Middle East, there may well be no permanent solution for another fifty years, if ever. A patched-up peace between Egypt and Israel has created as many problems as it solved.

Israel is still, and will continue to be, harassed by

Palestinian terrorists, and Egypt has won the eternal enmity of her Arab neighbors for having made peace with Israel.

So it is with human relationships. Sometimes there is no simple solution.

I recall the case of a woman crippled by rheumatoid arthritis. She had a pleasant but controlling husband. A few months after he died, she was completely cured of her ailment. The quiet repression of her resentment had brought on the arthritis; relief came only when he was gone. Her entire personality changed, and she became a radiant, cheerful person.

I also remember a very gentle young husband who, in a relatively few years, became a passive, hopeless failure as the result of being beaten down by a critical, over-bearing, demanding wife. It can work both ways.

THE FIRST HARD LESSON

There is a Sufi story in which Nasrudin asks a music teacher how much he will charge to teach him to play the flute.

"Ten gold pieces for the first lesson," replied the master, "and one gold piece for each lesson thereafter."

"In that case," replied Nasrudin, "I'll start with the second lesson."[2]

The story points up our very human reluctance to avoid the costly first lesson. In the case of human relationships, it is learning how to acquire patience, understanding, wisdom—a whole gamut of new skills. Difficult? Yes. But it is well worth the effort.

When you're interested in what you're doing
—whether it's running a country newspaper
or a grocery store or practicing psychiatry or
writing a novel—if it's not criminal, you're a
successful human animal, whether your
name is a household word throughout the
land or unknown thirty miles away.

—*H. B. Fox*

---

11 • Formula for Failure— and Success

Let's consider some simple, down-to-earth steps—
"ten sure ways"—guaranteed to destroy relationships. Over the years I have observed many people using
these methods with remarkable effectiveness.

1. *Never compromise.*

If you cherish your own methods and ideas, stick to
your guns. Don't give in. Not only in matters of morality
and integrity, but where methods are concerned, stand
firm!

I watched an otherwise intelligent, gifted man lose
four splendid positions in a row and end up bankrupt
because he never learned to distinguish between principles and methods. He fought as earnestly for a simple
procedure as he would have for some great moral principle. Because he was uncompromising, he was a failure.

2. *Compromise too often.*

Those people who have a vast need to please, and not
enough backbone, often tend to compromise too much.

They will give in on almost anything in order to avoid a confrontation.

Stanley had an inordinate need to please. Having received little love as a child, he was willing in adulthood to go to any lengths to win approval. He was the original "yes man," in favor of whatever anyone else was for. He always reflected the opinion of the last person he talked to. Stanley managed to earn a living in a minor capacity in a large corporation where he was given routine responsibilities requiring no initiative.

3. Get even!

Don't let people get away with anything. If you are attacked, retaliate. If you are criticized, tell them off! Or, if you dislike face-to-face encounters, round up as many friends or associates as you can; tell them how badly you were treated and get them on your side. This way, even though you will be a disruptive factor at work or in your social group, you won't have taken it lying down.

Once several leading members of a church that had no pastor at the time called me in for some advice on how to resolve a serious problem. The leaderless church was being torn asunder by gossip. Two groups had been pitted against each other by some wild rumors. No one seemed to know who had started the rumors, but all agreed that the church would die if the situation continued.

Having neither time nor inclination to try to turn up the culprit(s), I asked the group to spend some time in silent prayer. I said, "The problem person may be someone who is sincere and possibly devout, but very dangerous. We will not try to find out who it is, only pray for a solution." After the period of silent prayer, I closed, asking God's guidance and intervention.

The next day one of the women phoned me excitedly: "Something has happened! Some of us suspected one of the women in the church as the source of the false rumors, but we didn't want to make any accusations. This morning I learned that her husband has suddenly been transferred. Could this be the answer to our prayer?"

I said, "Let's see if things quiet down."

They did. Almost miraculously, a great peace descended on the congregation. The source of infection had been removed. We could only hope that this woman would not repeat her performance in another church.

Investigation revealed that she had felt severely criticized by another member of the church. In an effort to get even, she had lined up as many people as she could and initiated rumors about her "enemy." Thus sides were drawn, and all manner of damage was done to the congregation. Of course, such people are emotionally ill and desperately in need of psychotherapy.

Vengeance is the sweetest morsel ever brewed in hell. It may feel good to get even, but hate is the most corrosive of all emotions. It is like an acid that corrodes the vessel that contains it.

4. *Make yourself feel superior by tearing people down.*

The chief reason people become excessively critical is in order to feel superior. If you can find someone to criticize, you get a momentary feeling of superiority. But it is a psychological axiom that the most critical person feels the most inferior. Such individuals are usually avoided by all except their own kind.

Gwen, an ardent church member, was quite rigid in her doctrinal beliefs. Unfortunately, her sweetly sad criticism of her minister's theology attracted a small coterie of other women whose legalistic views mirrored hers. Her critical attitude divided the church. Feeling somewhat inferior because of her lack of formal education, she gained temporary status with her "biblically based" attacks on her minister.

5. *Learn how to attack.*

The best defense is a good offense, which explains why some people are so offensive.

Here is a ready-made list for husbands and wives:

"You never take me anyplace."

"You never help me with the housework."

"All you ever do is watch TV."

"Why don't you ever help me with the kids?"

"All you ever do is nag."

"What do you *do* all day?"

"Money doesn't grow on trees!"

"You're not the same person I married."

"Why can't you be more like . . . ?"

And for use with children (raise your voice with these):

"Look what you did!"

"If you do that one more time . . ."

"Stop that this instant!"

"What are we ever going to *do* with you?"

"Just wait until your father gets home."

This approach is guaranteed to make a hell out of a haven.

6. *Give lots of advice.*

If you think people are off base, tell them so. Let them know exactly what you think they should do. How will they ever know unless you tell them? Don't let the fact that they resent unsolicited advice stop you. You have a moral obligation to spread your wisdom and insight over as wide an area as possible. The fact that others seem unable to profit from your advice only shows how foolish people can be.

7. *Tell it like it is.*

Don't pussyfoot around; have the courage of your convictions. Let people know exactly where you stand. If you lose some friends, that's just tough. If they can't take it, it's their problem.

Don't mollycoddle people; tact is soft soap. Be absolutely frank and honest all the time. If you think the neighbors aren't raising their kids right, tell them so. Give them the benefit of your experience. Somebody has to tell them. Don't mince words. You may be very lonely, but that's the price you have to pay if you are really honest.

8. *If you have a legitimate complaint, keep it to yourself.*

Don't ever let anyone know if you have a valid complaint; keep it to yourself. You don't want to hurt anyone else's feelings, so sit on your own. Even if you share your complaint ever so tactfully, they might not like you, and you'd lose a friend. Or someone might get mad at you.

(Numbers 7 and 8 are two extremes. Both are fatal to relationships.)

9. *Try to get everyone to agree with you.*

When you find someone who disagrees with you on anything—religion, politics, or the way things are done in your group—set them straight. You see things more clearly than they do, and they need to have the proper facts set before them. Don't give up. Stick to your guns. If you lose the argument and a friend in the process, that's just the way the cookie crumbles.

10. *Wait for people to speak to you. Don't stick your neck out.*

Lots of people aren't all that friendly. If they don't speak to you first, don't bother with them. Some folks are just like that. Don't introduce yourself; let others take the first step. If they want to make friends, let them start. Why should you be the one who always has to take the initiative?

FAMILY FIGHTS

Dr. Wayne W. Dyer says of family arguments:

Virtually all fights revolve around the erroneous thought, "If only you were more like me, I wouldn't have to be upset." This is erroneous because people will never be the way you want them to be; you are really saying to yourself, "If only you were thinking the way I am thinking right now, I wouldn't have to be so upset," or "Why can't you do things the way I want them done?"[1]

He then lists twenty different types of things people fight about in the home. They are

— The checking account
— Your room is not clean
— Taking out the garbage
— Doing household chores
— Visiting parents
— Attending parties, funerals, weddings
— Doing the dishes
— Too many bills
— Where to go on holidays
— You keep your feelings to yourself
— You're late again
— Your past behavior (The affair you had last year. You didn't paint the house last spring.)
— Personality variables (You're too shy, lazy, clumsy, aggressive, fearful, etc.)
— You're not the person I married
— I want more freedom
— You're inconsiderate
— Drinking, smoking, and other personal habits
— You're not doing your homework
— You embarrass me
— I've no time to myself . . . I want privacy[2]

Some of these may seem like trifles; but three trifles make one pretty good beef, five can precipitate a fight, and ten will bring on a crisis.

SCREAMING PARENTS

A young mother said to me in a counseling session, "I just *hated* the way my mother screamed at us. I resolved that when I became a mother I was going to be patient and understanding. Now I hear myself screaming at my children just the way she yelled at me; and when I'm fed up with my kids, I get mean and angry at my husband. Then he yells back at me. What kind of examples are we to our children? Why do we act like that when we know better?"

WRITING ABOUT LOVE—OR LIVING IT

Tolstoy was the man who always talked about living the life of love. But his wife wrote poignantly of him, "There is so little genuine warmth about him; his kind-

168

ness does not come from his heart, but merely from his principles. His biographies will tell of how he helped the laborers to carry buckets of water, but no one will know that he never gave his wife a rest and never—in all these thirty-two years—gave his child a drink of water or spent five minutes by his bedside to give me a chance to rest a little from all my labors."[3]

THE LOVE PRINCIPLE

Most Christians are familiar with 1 Corinthians 13:4–7 and 13. Here is how it is paraphrased in *The Living Bible:*

> Love is very patient and kind, never jealous or envious, never boastful nor proud, never haughty nor selfish nor rude. Love does not demand its own way. It is not irritable or touchy. It does not hold grudges and will hardly even notice when others do it wrong. It is never glad about injustice, but rejoices whenever truth wins out. If you love someone you will be loyal to him no matter what the cost. You will always believe in him, always expect the best of him, and always stand your ground in defending him. . . . There are three things—faith, hope and love—that keep on forever; but the greatest of these is love.

Millions of devout people who believe earnestly in that lofty principle have found it difficult to live up to it. The critical comment, the carping attitude, the unloving response slip out before they can be checked.

I don't think much of a conversion experience that doesn't convert the tongue. A screaming wife/mother and a shouting, angry husband/father are wretchedly poor examples of basic Christianity. Children who learn about love and tolerance on Sunday but live with the opposite six days a week are going to be influenced most by what they experience at home. What children are *told* doesn't have as much effect as what they observe.

THE STEPS TO SUCCESS

Success must be defined in terms of your goals. A man whose ambition in life is to run a bait shop near the beach could consider himself a success if he attained that goal. If, on the other hand, he were determined to earn a million dollars by the age of thirty and amassed only seven hundred thousand dollars, he might feel like a failure.

A woman aspiring to become a beautician, and ultimately to own her own shop, would consider herself a success if she achieved that goal. But if she didn't realize her ambition to write a best-selling novel, she would label herself a failure.

Don't buy the marketplace standard of success, which defines it only in terms of money, fame, or possessions. Set your own goals.

A friendless, emaciated old man, suffering badly from malnutrition and driven half out of his mind by terrifying phobias, died a few years ago. Howard Hughes was one of the richest men in the world. Would anyone term him a success now?

A young movie star/sex symbol of the fifties whose name was known around the world committed suicide at the peak of her career. Until that fateful moment, millions of women would have loved to trade places with her. Marilyn Monroe had been a badly mistreated orphan whose beauty had thrust her to the pinnacle of a success she couldn't handle.

In glancing through a *New Yorker* magazine in a doctor's office, I noted a large advertisement that read: "When you stay at one of our hotels, you have arrived." Success by this standard is based upon which hotel you choose.

Lin Yutang wrote, "After allowances are made for the necessity of having a few supermen in our midst—explorers, conquerers, great inventors, great presidents, heroes who change the course of history—the happiest man is still the man of the middle class who has earned a slight measure of economic independence, who has done a little, but just a little, for mankind, and who is slightly distinguished in his community, but not too distinguished."[4]

When will you have attained success?

When you have lost thirty pounds? Been a good parent? Acquired that new house? Won a longed-for promotion? Gotten out of debt? Overcome a set of bad habits? When your children have grown up and you've been around the world? When you've written a book and retired to Florida?

Whatever your specific ambitions in life, taking the following ten steps will help you become a more successful person.

1. *Judge others with kindness.*

We usually judge ourselves by our ideals and others by their actions. There is a vast discrepancy between the two. G. B. White deals with this tendency in a whimsical manner:

"I am neat and orderly; you are a little officious; he is a fussbudget.

"My dog is outgoing and friendly, yours is a public nuisance; theirs will hear from my lawyer.

"I don't intend killing myself working; you are a little slack; he is a deadbeat.

"I had a disagreement with the IRS; you used some questionable deductions; he was busted by the Feds."[5]

Jesus issued a startling injunction: "Judge not, that you be not judged. For with the judgment you pronounce you will be judged, and the measure you give will be the measure you get."[6]

This means that if I am harsh in my evaluation of people, I will be judged by the same critical yardstick. I will be dealt with gently on Judgment Day only if I have been generous in my judgments of people. If I want leniency in the final reckoning, I must exhibit that attitude in my dealings with people here on earth.

When I observe someone whose conduct is despicable, it sobers me to consider that if I had been born of his or her parents, had the same genes, and had experienced life precisely as he or she has, I might be just like him or her.

Abraham Lincoln put it rather succinctly. According to Herndon, his biographer and law partner, Lincoln once stated that, "No man is to be eulogized for what he does, or censured for what he did or did not do, since all of us are the children of condition, of circumstances, of environment, of education, of acquired habits and of heredity. . . ."[7] Speak gently of others. To know all is to forgive all.

2. *Remember to express gratitude, but don't expect it from others.*

An outstanding minister, pastor of a large and influential church, once told me that he had recommended twenty-seven different men for pastoral positions in various churches. In each instance, the man had been accepted. Not one of these people ever wrote to thank him.

Samuel Liebowitz, before he became a judge, was a famous criminal attorney. He once said that he had saved seventy-eight men from the electric chair. None of them ever bothered to thank him.

Jesus once healed ten lepers. Only one returned to express gratitude.

The above are not isolated instances, but rather a commentary on one aspect of human nature. As Dr. Samuel Johnson once said, "Gratitude is a fruit of great cultivation; you do not find it among gross people." If you help people, let virtue be its own reward. Do it for the satisfaction of lending a hand, but don't expect them to be grateful.

On the other hand, if someone has helped you—has been a good friend, or has lent a hand at a difficult time in your life—remember to thank that person. You will stand out if you do, because such expressions are fairly rare.

When you pray, how much of your time is spent *asking* and how much *thanking* God? It is not that God needs our gratitude, but that we reveal our littleness of spirit if we major in supplication and minor in thanksgiving.

Marcus Aurelius, one of the relatively few wise men to rule the Roman Empire, once wrote in his diary, "I am

going to be meeting people today who talk too much—
people who are selfish, egotistical, ungrateful. But I
won't be surprised or disturbed, for I can't imagine a
world without such people."

If you are going to give of yourself, do it for the sheer
joy of being helpful, and try not to recall whether the
recipients bothered to express their thanks.

3. *Learn to accept criticism without taking offense.*

Dale Carnegie, whose books have sold in the millions,
tells of the time early in his career when a reporter for
the New York *Sun* attended a demonstration meeting of
his adult education class and ridiculed his work. Says
Carnegie,

> "Was I burned up! I took it as a personal insult. I tele-
> phoned . . . the chairman of the Executive Committee of
> the *Sun*, and practically demanded that he print an article
> stating the facts, instead of ridicule.
>
> I was ashamed of the way I acted. I realize now that half of
> the people who bought the paper never saw the article. Half
> of those who read it regarded it as a source of innocent
> merriment, half of those who gloated over it forgot about it
> in a few weeks. . . .
>
> People are not thinking about you and me, or caring what
> is said about us. They are thinking about themselves—
> before breakfast, after breakfast, and right on until ten min-
> utes past midnight. They would be a thousand times more
> concerned about a slight headache of their own than they
> would about the news of your death or mine.[8]

Does criticism offend you unduly? Are you terribly upset
when misquoted and maligned? The only perfect human
who ever lived was betrayed by one of his disciples,
denied by another, doubted by a third, and misunder-
stood by all the others. The jealous religious leaders
not only criticized him; they insisted that his miracles of
healing were done through the power of Satan. At one
point in his ministry, we read, "Many of his disciples
drew back and no longer went about with him."[9] He was
"despised and rejected of men."[10] If all this could happen to Jesus, there is no particular reason why we should

expect to be free of criticism and rejection.

I have found it interesting to keep up with the popularity polls of the various presidents. There is no possible way any president can win the approval of the entire electorate. There will always be people who dislike or even hate him. If he is approved by 55 to 60 percent of the voters, he considers himself fortunate. The only possible way to avoid censure or misunderstanding is to slink into the shadows, express no opinions, and do your best to be ignored.

4. *Focus on the needs of other people.*

Remember that one fundamental human need is to feel significant.

Some years ago a large industrial firm conducted a series of experiments to determine how it could make the employees more productive. The workers, of course, were made aware of this. First a music system was installed. Productivity soared. After a few weeks the music was turned off. Efficiency increased still more. They then installed indirect lighting. Production improved. After a while the original lighting was restored. Production still went up.

In the next experiment, desks were rearranged in the interest of greater efficiency. Morale improved, and so did production. In a few weeks the desks were restored to their original position. There was another noticeable improvement in results.

This was baffling. No matter what the company did, the workers tended to improve their performance. Several more changes, major and minor, were made. In every instance, production increased and morale improved.

Finally the experimenters realized that it was not the changes they were making that brought about improved performance; it was the fact that *the employees were made to feel significant.*

The need to feel important is pointed up in a news item about a man who spent thirty-six days and nights in a ten-foot cage with deadly snakes. He did it, he explained, in an effort to get his name in the *Guinness Book of World Records*. In a world where most humans have little chance of becoming famous, people will do almost anything to be noticed. *Pay attention to people to make them feel significant.*

5. *Handle interruptions creatively.*

You are in the midst of something that is important to you, and you encounter a series of interruptions. Your time is limited, and you have deadlines to meet. Then other people intrude on your time. Unless you have the gift of limitless patience, you grow tense, then irritated, and finally exasperated. Parents get lots of this from small children. Everyone experiences it at times.

But the very frequency of your interruptions may be an indication of your value as a person. The only people who are interrupted are those whose life and work are of some significance. Interruptions are the evidence of your indispensability.

By nature I neither suffer fools gladly nor endure interruptions with infinite patience. Having my train of thought or schedule disturbed repeatedly saps my energy more than hours of work do. My head tells me that the people who intrude into my schedule have a right to do so—that they need me, or my response. But my emotions tell me that I am irritated beyond measure. This is a grave defect on my part. However, as I work on it, I find myself achieving modest gains.

6. *Learn the value of silence and brevity.*

There are "silver-tongued orators" (once very highly regarded), but it is still true that "silence is golden." There is great wisdom in knowing when to be still. Unfortunately, some never acquire it.

James Thom, in an article on "Taciturnity," says,

> We suggest an addition to the usual college speech-department curriculum; a course to teach people when to be still. It could be called Silence 101, or perhaps Basic Reticence, maybe Social Circumspection.
> For every time we regret keeping still, there are about ten

times we regret speaking up. Common reasons that words get us into trouble:

1) We don't express what we mean; 2) We speak at the wrong moment; 3) People react not to what we said but to what they thought we said.

In our non-speech course, we might quote Thomas Carlyle: "Speech is great, but silence is greater." And Plutarch: "He can never speak well, who knows not how to hold his peace." And we'd send our students away with the maxim: "A closed mouth gathers no foot."[11]

I recall a church business meeting where a controversial issue was being debated with considerable heat. A dozen or more people had spoken, some for and some against the proposal. Finally C. V. Johnson, a white-haired, benign, elderly member, arose slowly, put the tips of his fingers together, and, speaking softly and very slowly, said, "It is quite possible that I could be wrong, but. . . ." Then he launched into a thoughtful analysis of the issue. He saw virtue in the proposal but had some objections. In his very brief summation he clarified the matter, weighed the pros and cons, and said, "Therefore, I move that we reject the proposal on the aforementioned grounds." The vote was unanimous, and I thought, quite rightly so. This man had remained silent through two hours of debate, and shed light and wisdom on the matter in three minutes.

A friend of mine, in response to a harsh criticism, looked thoughtful and said, "Thank you. I appreciate that observation. I want to give it some thought." His critic was left openmouthed.

Silence or brevity can be a powerful response.

7. *Give a little extra.*

James E. Byrnes, secretary of state under Franklin D. Roosevelt, once said,

I discovered at an early age that most of the differences between average people and great people can be explained in three words—'and then some.'

The top people did what was expected of them, and then some. They were considerate and thoughtful of others, and then some. They met their obligations and responsibilities fairly and squarely, and then some. They were good friends to their friends, and then some. They could be counted on in an emergency, and then some.[12]

The most important single event in my life, aside from choosing my wife, was when I once offered to work for nothing.

I was the youngest, greenest student in the seminary. I already had two part-time jobs, but one day on a whim I dropped in to talk to the editor of a denominational journal. I told him I wanted to do some writing for him. He said, "Son, our budget is pretty tight, and we don't need another writer just now."

"I understand," I said, "but I don't expect to be paid. I just want to do some writing. I have a few ideas I want to try out."

"Sit down, young fellow. I want to talk to you. You're the first person who ever came in and offered to work for nothing. Bring me some samples of the type of thing you have in mind, and I'll consider it."

In a few days I presented him with some sample material. He liked it, and gave me, thereafter, two entire pages in every issue. A few months later he expressed interest in my future, took me downstairs to a denominational official, and said, "John, fix this young man up with a church. He needs some experience." Somehow he found a small church for me, and in the next two years I gained valuable experience I could never have gotten in any other way.

The "and then some" attitude is important. It can change your life, if applied as a lifelong principle.

8. *Work toward the goal of accepting—and loving—yourself.*

Proper self-love is not egotism. You are to love *yourself* as you love your neighbor. Not only are you *entitled* to love yourself; you are expected to do so. For you can love another person only to the degree that you love yourself.

I recall a young woman who had, in rebellion, dropped out of high school. Later she married a fine young man with considerable ability. They had a great deal of influence in their church. Unfortunately, because of her enormous inferiority complex and contentious nature, she was a very divisive influence. She became the focal point of gossip and dissension. Even her amiable husband got caught in it, in defending her. Her sweet veneer concealed a hostile, bitter spirit. She and her husband were virtually forced out of one church because of their divisiveness, and she managed to stir up serious trouble in another. Never having learned to love herself, she could not relate to another person without either intense possessiveness or vicious hostility.

Work toward the goal of accepting yourself—your liabilities, your strengths, your virtues and weaknesses. View your limitations with amused, friendly tolerance.

9. *Accept your emotions as valid.*

All of our feelings are valid. But many people, reared by nonaffirming parents or with a legalistic religious background, tend to reject certain feelings and label them as "bad."

The two strongest emotions God has given us are the sex drive and anger. Because of their strength and potential for destructiveness, society has set up rules and regulations to direct our sexuality and aggression into creative channels.

Many schools give some instruction regarding the biological aspect of sexuality. However, the emotional and spiritual side of the subject are often dealt with rather inadequately.

Few parents can handle the subject of sex easily and skillfully when discussing it with their children. But the proliferation of books on the subject is making this somewhat easier. All public libraries have books on human sexuality, and virtually every bookstore carries a wide selection of titles. Because of the importance of the sex drive, one should read extensively on the subject.

In our counseling center we have encountered an amazing fact: though most women have read widely on the subject of human sexuality, most men have read either little or nothing. There is a general male tendency to feel that "I know all about it," which is often far from the truth.

Anger is of God, divine in origin. We must accept our anger for what it is: a survival instinct. *Expressing* hostility may be either inappropriate or valid, depending upon the circumstances; but *feeling* the emotion of anger is normal. The New Testament puts it this way: "Be angry but do not sin. . . ."[13] Here is recognition of the fact that we will be angry at times. The verse continues, "Do not let the sun go down on your anger." In a subsequent verse we read, "Let all bitterness and wrath and anger and clamor and slander be put away from you, with all malice."[14] These things have to do with a vengeful, malicious, hostile attitude—not with the emotion of anger, which is normal.

Jesus was angry on more than one occasion. Paul and Barnabas had an argument so bitter that they had to part company, and Paul and Peter had a hot verbal encounter at Jerusalem over an important issue.

Accept the fact that God has given you the capacity for anger, but *learn how to control it* so that it is not destructive.

Accept your other emotions—even the ones that seem negative—as normal human characteristics, too. If they are excessive, then you may need anything from self-control to intensive therapy. But accept the emotions themselves as realities. Because repression leads to obsession, refusal to accept your emotions can cause you to become obsessive or phobic.

10. *Accept life.*

Life isn't easy, as has been pointed out. No one ever said that it was going to be easy. But it is preferable to the alternative.

Acceptance does not imply approval. We don't have to *like* the difficulties we encounter, but we do have to accept them as given.

There are three important steps in resolving any

179

problem: *awareness, acceptance, and action.* Let's examine those three steps.

We must become *aware* of the problem before it can be resolved. This may mean getting in touch with deeper emotions rather than denying them. Never lie to yourself about your feelings. Denial solves nothing, and it can be very destructive.

Then, we must *accept* the situation. This need not involve liking it. I hate some aspects of life: murder, death, violence, poverty, hunger, injustice, war, and a lot of other things. But I accept them as a reality. I dislike certain aspects of my personality, but I have to acknowledge that I possess those traits.

Third, we must decide what *action* to take. This may involve analyzing the problem, learning discipline, laying long-range plans, or seeking counsel.

Although we may be victimized by the corporate sins of society, we can succeed if—throughout a lifetime—we recognize the laws that govern the universe. God wants you to be a successful person, and His power and love and guidance are available to help you achieve that goal.

Love all God's creation, both the whole and
every grain of sand. Love every leaf, every
ray of light. Love the animals, love the
plants, love each separate thing. If thou love
each thing thou will perceive the mystery of
God in all; and when once thou perceive this,
thou will henceforth grow every day to a ful-
ler understanding of it; until thou come at last
to love the whole world with a love that will
then be all-embracing and universal.

—*Feodor Dostoevsky*

12 • Facets of Love

I once told a group of people at a seminar, "We are not
responsible for one another. We are responsible to
express love *to* others, not to be responsible *for* them."

A woman interrupted and said, "What about the
teaching of Jesus about being our brother's keeper?"

I pointed out as gently as I could that Jesus said nothing about being anyone's keeper. "The quotation you are
referring to" I said, "is found in the Book of Genesis.
Cain had killed his brother Abel, and when God asked,
'Where is your brother?' Cain snarled, 'Am I my
brother's keeper?'" There was a moment's silence. Then
I asked the woman who had raised the question, "Do you
want someone to be *your* keeper?" She said emphati-
cally that she didn't.

HELPING AN ALCOHOLIC

An alcoholic named Bob kept showing up at my office
from time to time, asking for money for a night's lodging
and a meal. Feeling vague disquietude and mixed emo-

tions, I always gave him some money. But I knew that I was not solving his basic problem.

My secretary, whose husband was a recovered alcoholic, said to me one day, "You know, of course, that you aren't really helping him, don't you?"

"Yes, but I don't know what else to do. He refuses to go to AA. When he comes here hungry and homeless, what can I do?"

"You would be acting more in love if you refused him," she replied. "He will never recover until he is scared and totally desperate. He has to hit bottom first."

I knew she was right. The next time Bob came around, I told him gently but firmly that I was sorry, but I couldn't do a thing for him except drive him to an alcoholic rehabilitation center. He cursed me angrily and left.

I had not been helping Bob with my handouts. I had been mistakenly *trying to be responsible for him,* on a short-range basis, instead of expressing love on a long-range basis.

Later I learned that Bob, hungry and desperate, had begged fare to San Francisco, twenty miles away. Failing to panhandle more funds there, he had turned himself in at an alcoholic rehab institution. He soon got a job, saved his money, and took a bus back to his home in Georgia.

Kindly and compassionate people can often be manipulated into feeling responsible for people who really aren't their responsibility.

HELP ON YOUR TERMS

If you want to help people, *do it on your own terms.* Only you know how much time, energy, sympathy, or money you have available.

Having been raised to be rather compliant, I felt obligated for many years to meet the needs of anyone who asked me for help. Some vague but powerful inner force kept me from saying "no" to people. I have had people ask me, "What are you doing tomorrow night?" and then look over my shoulder while I glanced at my date book. I always resented this, but it still required a genuine effort on my part to refuse the request.

I finally learned a way of avoiding the "no" and at the same time rejecting the request if it were not convenient from a wise and tactful older friend. This man was a loving, gentle person whom everyone admired. He never took on more than he could conveniently handle, yet he never said "no" to anyone. Smiling warmly, he would either acquiesce or say, "I'd *love* to, but I'm already committed on that date."

I suspected that, on occasion, the engagement was with his wife or a good book, though he was involved in many activities and gave of himself generously. But he knew when and how to keep from overextending himself. Though I still find myself overcommitted at times, I cannot begin to calculate the innumerable engagements I have been able to turn down by using my friend's formula: "I'd love to, but. . . ."

Jesus refused, in love, to listen to his mother and brothers on one occasion. They had pressed through the crowd as far as they could get, then sent a messenger to tell him they wanted to talk to him. Told that his mother and brothers wanted to see him, he said, "Who is my mother? Who are my brothers? . . . the person who does what my Father in heaven wants him to do is my brother, my sister, my mother."[1]

Love does not imply being responsible *for* people. We are simply to love them, care about them, and do whatever seems indicated under the circumstances.

DOCTORS AND THEIR ATTITUDES

Dr. David Wheatley, an English physician, studied a group of patients suffering from acute anxiety. They were being treated by different physicians, all of whom were using similar tranquilizers.

The best results were observed in those patients whose physicians were basically optimistic and encouraging. Somewhat poorer results were obtained in the case of the patients who were seeing physicians who were relatively indifferent. Extremely poor results were observed in patients whose doctors exhibited a considerable degree of pessimism regarding the outcome. In other words, the attitude of the attending physician seemed to play an important part in the patient's cure. The tranquilizers produced some results, but the most important ingredient was the attitude of the doctors who cared genuinely; for *caring* is a *facet* of love.

DOCTORS WHO KEEP YOU WAITING

I once made an appointment for a regular physical examination with a doctor who had been highly recommended. At the doctor's office I was kept waiting forty minutes, after which I told the receptionist that I had another engagement and would have to come back another time. She gave me another appointment.

The next time I was kept waiting twenty-five minutes. I began to be a bit irritated, as I considered my time quite as valuable as the doctor's. I announced to the receptionist that I would have to come another day, as I had allotted only so much time for the visit. She told me that it might be best to schedule the next appointment immediately after lunch, as the doctor would be returning from lunch at precisely 1:00. I agreed.

A week later at one o'clock, I was in the waiting room. At 1:15 I rose and told the receptionist that I was sorry, but I couldn't wait any longer. As I started out of the office toward the parking lot, she came running after me: "He's just coming up the walk now."

I glanced down the sidewalk. The physician was very, very leisurely sauntering up to the door of the building. I looked at my watch. It was 1:18. I said, "Tell him I am going to find another physician."

FUMING IN THE WAITING ROOM

Though this type of doctor is in the minority, there are some who show a lack of consideration for the patient's time. Being forced to sit for twenty to forty minutes in a waiting room, with nothing to read but ancient copies of *Time* and *Newsweek*, does little for one's peace of mind—unless, of course, one is grateful to get away from the job and rest for a bit, or to escape from the incessant demands of small children. Or unless one is like my wife,

Isobel, who has the gift of infinite patience with neurotic or irrational behavior.

What has this to do with getting along with people? A great deal. People are grossly irritated, and often made very angry, by having to wait. To steal time is tantamount to stealing money or property. There is very little difference.

If you genuinely care—and caring is an important aspect of love—about another person's well-being, you will be considerate enough to be consistently on time. Obviously there are those occasional emergencies which make this impossible; but to be a latenik—perpetually late—says to the one waiting, "I don't really care about your having had to wait. My time is more important than yours."

GIVING AND RECEIVING COMPLIMENTS

New Testament love—*agape*—does not necessarily have the connotation of liking or of affection. We have no English word that precisely encompasses its meaning, but it can be described as *unconditional positive concern for the well-being of another*.

With this in mind, a loving person—in the *agape* sense of the word—will be free with compliments. *You* want to be loved, *you* want to be complimented, *you* are waiting to be affirmed—and so is everyone else. So, if you want to be genuinely appreciated, be free with well-deserved compliments. Most people have been criticized so much that they are not likely to suffer from an excess of approval.

Compliments should never be followed by a "but."

"You usually do such a good job, but I was a little disappointed this time because . . ."

"That's a lovely outfit, but do you think it's just the right thing to wear at . . ."

It is much easier to handle sincere praise or honest criticism alone than a mixture of the two.

Many people have difficulty receiving compliments gracefully. Often they feel a need to reciprocate: "Thank you. I'm glad you like it, but yours is lovely, too." It is not necessary to respond in kind; "thank you" is quite adequate.

INTELLECT AND EMOTIONS

We humans operate far more on the emotional level than on the intellectual. The intellect explains what the emotions decide, for the intellect is but a speck in an ocean of emotion.

Because we are motivated more by our feelings than by facts, you will have better relationships if you *make people feel good about themselves*. Let's consider some common mistakes people make that cause others to feel badly about themselves.

Criticism is very destructive. In fact, almost all criticism, no matter how carefully expressed, is perceived by the recipient as an attack. We may intend to be constructive, and even label it as that, but it nearly always feels destructive to the one being criticized.

Jack Denton Scott once said,

> A wise parent makes it a point to compliment a child when he deserves it. A woman I know has a twelve-year-old son who considers drying dishes for his mother a great honor. It came about by way of a compliment. One night he was grudgingly drying a large meat platter when it slipped and crashed to the floor. Silence. Then his mother said, "Robert, of all the times you have dried dishes for me, this is the first time you dropped one. I think you have set some kind of a record." Anxiety left the boy's face and he grinned. Thereafter, he never complained about having to dry the dishes. As one psychologist advises: "Commend virtue and you will have few vices to condemn."[2]

Children desperately need to be complimented, but adults need it, too. One of the deepest human needs is to feel important. People thrive better on compliments than on criticism.

One should never, never criticize another person in public, or even offer a mildly disparaging remark. If you want to be genuinely loathed, practice the murderous art of demeaning people in public. If someone needs to be corrected, always do it in private.

Diplomacy as a Facet of Love

Benjamin Franklin, that wise old colonial philosopher, scientist, and diplomat, had quite a bit to say about tact, for he was a master of it. It was because of his tactfulness that he was sent to France as a special diplomat.

Franklin pointed out that it is wise not to be dogmatic, but rather to prefix one's statements with such phrases as, "It is quite possible that I am wrong, but. . . ." Dogmatism irritates people and ruffles their feathers. It is counterproductive. The listener is less likely to agree with a dogmatic utterance than with one expressed tactfully.

Focusing on Others as a Facet of Love

Another aspect of *agape* involves letting the other person feel important. Calling attention to your achievements, your attainments, your possessions, can arouse envy. If you want to make friends, focus attention on others' accomplishments.

I was attending a social function and was seated next to a very friendly man. We were likely to be together for the next hour or so, so I asked him about his hobbies. He told me that he was interested in genealogies. Now, one of the least fascinating things in the world, to me, is who begat whom. Nevertheless, in the interest of being friendly, I asked him to tell me about his genealogical research. For an hour and a quarter he did so, quite oblivious to a musical rendition or two being performed at the other end of the room.

I wasn't greatly interested in the information, but I found the man fascinating. He had traveled extensively in the interest of his research, and to many countries I had visited; so we shared impressions. Mostly I asked questions. All in all, it was an interesting hour and a quarter.

I found it significant that at no time during our discussion did this man ask about my occupation or hobbies, or anything else about me. He was totally immersed in his own interests. I would not call this an ideal characteristic, but it is a normal human tendency.

What would I have gained by telling this man of my travels over the past thirty-five years? I would have derived no particular satisfaction from informing him of my interests or experiences. I was primarily concerned that we have a pleasant conversation. And I did learn something.

An important aspect of tact is the ability to draw people out, to let them talk. If you have deep feelings of inferiority and insecurity, you may have a great need to inform, to instruct, to grab the conversation. But what advantage will you gain in doing so?

SHOWING PEOPLE UP

There is usually very little to be gained by showing people where they are wrong. I can think of some instances in the past when I have mistakenly done so.

At a seminar I was conducting, a woman challenged some statement I had made and tried to prove, by quoting the apostle Paul, that women were to be obedient and subordinate to their husbands—rather surprising in this day and age. I spent considerable time enlightening her, only she didn't want to be enlightened. She was adamant. I succeeded only in alienating her. I am certain that this woman didn't hear another thing I said during the weekend. She was convinced that I didn't believe in the Bible.

A more tactful approach would have been to respond with, "You feel, then, that all of Paul's teachings about women two thousand years ago apply to domestic relations in our culture today?" I could have affirmed her without agreeing with her particular interpretation of the Scriptures. She had a perfect right to her convictions.

CHRISTIAN LOVE INVOLVES FORGIVENESS

I doubt if one can be a loving person without being forgiving.

There is a story about an old farmer who had been feuding with a neighbor for—as he put it—"nigh onto thirty years." The old gentleman knew that he was on his deathbed. Being in a quiet and mellow mood, he asked his wife to summon the neighbor.

When his ancient enemy had seated himself, the dying man said in a weak and trembling voice, "Abner, you and me has been feudin' about the fence line nigh onto thirty years. I've said some pretty hard things about you, and I want to tell you I'm mighty sorry. I'd jest like to be friends with you before I die. Will you forgive me?"

Abner was touched, and allowed as how he'd be mighty glad to do just that. The two shook hands.

Then the old man heaved himself up on one elbow, shook his finger, and said grimly, "But mind you, Abner, if I get well, you can fergit what I just said!"

Jesus made it clear that God cannot forgive us if we do not forgive others from the heart. That means, of course, from the depths of our being, at a deep emotional level. This is not as easy to do as it sounds.

In Primal Integration therapy, a young married woman began to relive various forgotten aspects of her childhood. She had no conscious memories of any traumatic events, but her emotional symptoms had suggested that there were some buried memories still troubling her.

Day after day she relived the pain of a too-busy father and a cold, unfeeling mother who assured her, "You know how much we love you, dear." The hurt and anguish of never being held or cuddled, of going to bed in a far corner of the house, of feeling hurt and angry and afraid and not knowing why, came out with tears and pleas:

"Mommy, please hold me; don't look at me like that . . ."

"Daddy, can I sit on your lap? . . ."

"I don't want to go to school, because nobody likes me; they hate me . . ."

And on and on, day after day, until her pain-filled childhood had been relived.

Then she exploded with anger at her parents. The uninhibited rage she expressed had been fueled by years of emotional starvation by two unfeeling, untouching parents. After hours of expressing that rage, she wept again: "But Mommy, Daddy, I love you. I'm sorry you can't love me; I understand." Then silence.

Finally, in her adult state, she said, "I can see now that they were incapable of loving anyone. I don't ache for their love any more. I feel vastly relieved, cleansed. It's as though a lifetime of hurt and anger have been discharged. I feel that I've forgiven them at last. I can sense how badly they were damaged by their parents. I even love them now. They did their best. What a relief!"

Then she added, "I thought I'd forgiven them years ago, and I guess I had to the best of my ability. But I sense now that it was an intellectual forgiveness, and not from the bottom of my heart." Primal Integration was a deeply religious and healing experience for her.

THE GUILTY CANNOT LOVE FULLY

Phyllis, a professional woman, was kind, gentle, helpful, eminently ethical and moral—and hurting. Without knowing precisely what she was looking for, she entered Primal Integration therapy and made a fantastic discovery.

Phyllis had described herself as excessively passive and hopelessly overcompliant. This tendency made her very unhappy, but she had been unable to rid herself of the compulsion to do everyone's bidding.

In one of her early primal sessions Phyllis relived the death of her younger brother, for which she had felt responsible. Feeling left out and neglected because of the birth of this brother, Phyllis had wished him dead.

To the child under the age of six, it is quite difficult to distinguish fantasy from fact. At that tender age Phyllis didn't know what "dead" meant; she just wanted her brother gone, out of the way, for he had taken her place. When he died, she felt that she had killed him.

In one session she screamed to her parents, "I'll be good, I'll be perfect. I'll do anything you say. I'll never be bad again!" And from that moment she never disobeyed, never rebelled—even during adolescence. Her passivity had been fixated at age five when she felt the enormity of her "crime." As an adult she was literally incapable of disobeying or displeasing another person. Her childhood vow was being lived out in adult life.

Phyllis's "guilt" was finally resolved through her therapy. That it was false guilt had not diminshed her unconscious need for self-punishment; one's emotional structure does not distinguish real guilt from false.

THE DEPRESSED CANNOT LOVE

Many of the people who come to the Burlingame Counseling Center from various parts of the United States and from foreign countries are suffering from depression.

Arlene was a smiling depressive who was having difficulty in her marriage.

At one point in her therapy she had told me that she disliked clowns. I asked her, "Could it be that you wear a false face, like a clown, and that behind the big painted smile you are crying?" She didn't think so.

Then I told her the famous story of the man in the psychiatrist's office who was deeply depressed. At the close of the session, the psychiatrist said, "Before our next session, I'd like for you to go to the circus. There's a marvelous clown there. He's called Toto the Clown. Let's see if his act won't cheer you up."

The man said, with infinite sadness, "I *am* Toto the Clown."

Arlene looked startled for a moment, then began to cry. She, too, was Toto the Clown, with a pretty, bright facade and a deep inner hurt.

In discharging her Primal Pain, she became able to function more normally again for the first time in several years.

HOW MANY PEOPLE CARE IF YOU LIVE OR DIE?

How many people genuinely, deeply care whether *you* live or die—apart, that is, from your immediate family?

There is usually a correlation between the number of people you love and the number who love you. We don't love others indiscriminately; we tend to love those who are lovable. If you make it a practice to affirm people and express goodwill, you will be lovable, and therefore loved. Jesus' dictum, "Give, and it will be given to you,"[3] has a distinct bearing on the matter of giving love. You must give it to receive it.

What Real Love Is

To "love" abstractions—such as peace, starving multitudes, or all of humanity—is relatively easy. To love those who love us is even easier. It's loving that miserable person next door that is the real problem. How can you love the wife beater, the malicious gossip, the arrogant snob, the blatant hypocrite? These are the kinds of people Jesus was talking about when he said, "Love your enemies." An enemy is anyone toward whom you feel enmity.

The kind of love Jesus commands is not an emotion. It has nothing to do with liking or affection. What we are called on to express to such insufferable people is unconditional goodwill. We all know that isn't easy. But no matter how doctrinally pure you may be, how much you love the Word of God, or how virtuous your life is, you have no right to boast about your religion unless you are making an effort to love the unlovable people of the earth—especially the ones who have injured you.

Christianity is not merely a matter of beliefs, but of obeying the specific commands of Jesus, such as, "Love your enemies, bless those who curse you, and pray for those who despitefully use you."[4] Believing is not enough. It is action, and right attitude that Jesus commanded.

When you have begun to take Jesus seriously and have learned to express love as He commanded, you will not only be one of His beloved disciples; you will find yourself getting along with and being loved by those around you. Isn't that what you really want?

Appendix

More than six million Americans received some form of psychotherapy in a recent year, despite growing evidence that "psychiatry does *no more good than placebos, or the passage of time.*"[1]

A ten-year study in New York City, *Mental Health In The Metropolis*, claimed that "approximately 80 percent of adults showed some symptoms of mental illness, with one in four actually impaired."[2]

The President's Commission on Mental Health stated that one-quarter of all Americans suffer from severe emotional stress, and warned that up to thirty-two million Americans are in need of professional psychiatric help.

Cut those figures in half, if you want to be ultraconservative, and they still represent an enormous number of people in need of some kind of therapy.

More alarming is the fact that numerous psychiatrists themselves are admitting that Freudian-oriented psychotherapy is "no more scientific than phrenology or astrology."[3] That statement was made by Dr. Alfred M. Freedman, head of the psychiatric department of the

New York Medical College and former president of the American Psychiatric Association.

A *Time* magazine cover story stated:

> The symptoms of psychiatry's ills are apparent enough. The U.S. has 27,000 psychiatrists in active practice, up from 5,800 in 1950. But now the bloom is off the therapeutic rose. Today only 4% to 5% of medical school graduates go into psychiatry, vs. 12% in 1970. Says one doctor, "Psychiatry is not where the action is." And if psychiatry is a medical treatment, why can its practitioners not provide measurable scientific results like those obtained by other doctors?
>
> Psychiatrists themselves acknowledge that their profession often smacks of modern alchemy . . . full of jargon, obfuscation and mystification, but precious little real knowledge. The Patty Hearst trial was a typical embarrassment . . . one battery of distinguished psychiatrists neatly explained that Hearst was ill, another insisted that she was not.
>
> Psychiatrist Eugene E. Levitt believes that psychotherapy is effective in approximately one in five cases. Dr. Paul E. Meehl, former president of the American Psychological Association, says that "only a small percentage of patients benefit from therapy, . . . and our present power to help is in reality quite limited."[4]

Such statements as these are echoed by Dr. O. Hobart Mowrer, former president of the American Psychological Association. He has pointed out that Freud himself, before he died, admitted that the therapeutic effectiveness of psychotherapy is poor, and that it was mainly a research tool.

In recent years at least a dozen or more studies have been conducted by psychiatrists in an effort to discover how effective members of their profession are. Without exception they have found that placebos (sugar pills) or time prove as effective as psychiatric care.

Martin Gross cites a chilling example of psychiatry's biases:

> Two psychologists at the University of Oklahoma employed an actor to play the part of a man of exceptional mental health. He manifested only very minor anxieties,

such as disagreements with his wife about churchgoing and certain aspects of childrearing. The researchers tape-recorded an interview with the actor and played the tape for two different groups of psychiatrists.

The first group was told that the patient lived in a $14,000 home, and earned $85 per week.

Another was told that the man had two magnificent homes, one in San Francisco and another in Tulsa. He was supposedly a wealthy industrialist, had attended a private school, and had done graduate work at Stanford University.

Unfortunately, psychiatric diagnosis was not by symptomatology, but by social class. The group which had been told the story of his low economic status diagnosed him as mentally ill, with rather poor prognosis.

The psychiatrists who heard the "wealthy" fabrication found him quite normal. When the hoax was admitted, the psychiatrists were astounded at their incredibly poor performance.[5]

Records show that the suicide rate among psychiatrists is *seven times that of the general population.*

There are now somewhat more than *one hundred different types of psychotherapy,* ranging from the standard Freudian-oriented approach to the nude bathing technique. Unfortunately, studies have revealed no evidence that any one of the standard approaches is better than another. On the basis of the findings of psychiatric researchers themselves, it is safe to say that fifty years from now the Freudian approach will be quite dead.

Some studies have shown that certain types of meditation, if *practiced consistently,* will relieve many physical and emotional symptoms temporarily. However, when the meditation approach is stopped, symptoms recur.

Since 1957, Yokefellows, Inc. has helped some seventy thousand persons achieve emotional and spiritual growth. The process involves a group approach, using psychological inventories to discover the personality barriers. There are groups in all fifty states, but not in every city.[6]

For persons with deeply buried personality problems, Primal Integration is by far the most effective method.[7] This involves reliving the buried traumas of childhood with as much intensity as the original event. This is accomplished without hypnosis or drugs. Long buried primal hurts, which distort the personality and prevent the developing of creative relationships, are reexperienced and integrated into the adult personality.

Now You Can Stop Hurting, by Dr. Cecil G. Osborne (Word Books, 1980), explains the process in considerable detail.

Notes

CHAPTER ONE

1. *Reader's Digest* (September 1978).
2. James T. Fisher, *A Few Buttons Missing: The Case Book of a Psychiatrist* (Philadelphia: Lippincott, 1951).
3. Matthew 5:7, 9, 21–25, 38–39, 43–45; 6:3–4; 7:1–2, 12 TEV.

CHAPTER TWO

1. The address of the Burlingame Counseling Center is 19 Park Road, Burlingame, CA 94010.
2. John 16:12 LB.
3. Mark 15:4 LB.
4. *Faith at Work.*
5. *Guideposts* (September 1978).
6. *Field Newspaper Syndicate* (27 April 1978).
7. Ephesians 4:15 RSV.
8. *San Francisco Chronicle* (7 May 1978).
9. John D. MacDonald, *A Deadly Shade of Gold* (Greenwich, Conn.: Fawcett, 1978).

CHAPTER THREE

1. Jack Denton Scott, "Count Your Compliments," in *Reader's Digest* (April 1976).

CHAPTER FOUR

1. *Human Nature* (June 1978).
2. Ibid.
3. *Faith at Work* (September 1976).
4. Ibid.
5. Ibid.
6. Ephesians 4:32 TEV.
7. "Pain" is capitalized because this kind of primal trauma must be distinguished from ordinary physical pain.
8. Mary Jo Bane, *Here to Stay: American Families in the Twentieth Century* (New York: Basic Books, 1978).
9. Ann Landers, in *Family Circle*.

CHAPTER FIVE

1. Nandor Fodor and Frank Gaynor, *Freud: Dictionary of Psychoanalysis* (Greenwich, Conn.: Fawcett, 1976).
2. Haim Ginott, *Between Parent and Child* (New York: Avon, 1973).
3. Ibid.
4. Ibid.
5. Matthew 16:18 RSV.
6. H. C. Caldwell, *Psychotherapy* (New York: Grove Press, 1968).
7. Dorothy C. Briggs, *Your Child's Self-Esteem: The Key to His Life* (Garden City, N.Y.: Doubleday, 1970).
8. Ibid.

CHAPTER SEVEN

1. Matthew 5:44 LB.
2. Wayne W. Dyer, *Pulling Your Own Strings* (New York: Funk and Wagnalls, 1978).

CHAPTER EIGHT

1. Manuel J. Smith, *When I Say No, I Feel Guilty* (New York: Bantam, 1975).

CHAPTER NINE

1. Ephesians 4:2 KJV.
2. Galatians 2:11 TEV.

3. Luke 11:9 TEV.
4. *Time* (March 1978).
5. Hans Selye, *Stress Without Distress* (Philadelphia: Lippincott, 1974).
6. Luke 12:48 RSV.

CHAPTER TEN

1. Psalm 19:12 RSV.
2. Edward E. Thornton, "Lord, Teach Us to Pray," in *Review and Expositor* (Spring 1979).

CHAPTER ELEVEN

1. Wayne W. Dyer, *Pulling Your Own Strings* (New York: Funk and Wagnalls, 1978).
2. Ibid.
3. William Barclay, *The Gospel of Luke,* The Daily Study Bible (Philadelphia: Westminster, 1953).
4. Lin Yutang, *The Importance of Living* (New York: Regnal and Hitchcock, 1937).
5. G. B. White, "On You, Me and Him," in *Reader's Digest* (April 1979).
6. Matthew 7:1–2 RSV.
7. William Herndon, *The Life of Lincoln* (New York: A. C. Boni, 1930).
8. Dale Carnegie, *How to Win Friends and Influence People* (New York: Pocket Books, 1977).
9. John 6:66 RSV.
10. Isaiah 53:3 KJV.
11. *Reader's Digest* (April 1979).
12. *Reader's Digest* (May 1979).
13. Ephesians 4:26 RSV.
14. Ephesians 4:31 RSV.

CHAPTER TWELVE

1. Matthew 12:48–50 TEV.
2. Bryan Jay Cannon, *Celebrate Yourself: The Secret to a Life of Hope and Joy* (Waco, Tex.: Word Books, 1977).
3. Luke 6:38 RSV.
4. Luke 6:27 RSV.

APPENDIX

1. Martin L. Gross, *The Psychological Society* (New York: Random House, 1978).

2. Ibid.
3. Ibid.
4. *Time* (2 April 1979).
5. Gross, *The Psychological Society.*
6. Yokefellows, Inc., 19 Park Road, Burlingame, CA 94010.
7. Therapists at the Burlingame Counseling Center, 19 Park Road, Burlingame, California (Dr. Cecil G. Osborne, Director) practice this therapy.